Sauces

Michel Roux

Sauces

Sweet and savory, classic and new

TRANSLATED AND
EDITED BY KATE WHITEMAN

PHOTOGRAPHS BY
MARTIN BRIGDALE

DEDICATION

The dedication of my newborn offspring *Sauces* needed only
a moment's reflection. Given that so few people have mastered this highly
important subject, I dedicate my "baby" to young cooks all over the world in the
hope that this book will help them to discover, master, and further develop the
wonderful, exhilarating world of sauces.

ACKNOWLEDGMENTS

My thanks go to the following people for their
invaluable contributions to this book: my son Alain Roux, first sous-chef at
The Waterside Inn, who tested all the recipes and prepared them for photography;
Martin Brigdale, whose superb photos brought them to life and Helen Trent who styled
them; Mary Evans for her artistic vision and her patience in tolerating my own artistic
temperament; Paul Welti for his excellent work on the design; Kate Whiteman, who
never fails to understand what I want to say even when I have forgotten to write all
the words; Claude Grant, who typed the manuscript day and night and cheerfully
coped with my illegible writing and impossible deadlines; and my wife Robyn,
who nurtures me through the creative process and continues
to put up with my little ways.

First published in the United States of America in 1996 by
Rizzoli International Publications Inc.
300 Park Avenue South, New York, NY 10010
www.rizzoliusa.com

Reprinted 2001, 2003 (twice), 2004, 2005

First published in Great Britain in 1996 by
Quadrille Publishing Ltd, London

Text copyright © Michel Roux 1996
Photography copyright © Martin Brigdale 1996
Design and layout © Quadrille Publishing Ltd 1996

Art director: Mary Evans
Design: Paul Welti
Publishing director: Anne Furniss
Project editor and translator: Kate Whiteman
American editor: Norma MacMillan
Styling: Helen Trent
Production: Vincent Smith

Library of Congress Cataloging-in-Publication Data

Roux, M ichel, 1941-
Michel Roux: Sauces/Michel Roux; photographs by Martin Brigdale.
p.   cm.
ISBN 0-8478-1970-1 (hardcover)
I. Sauces.   I. Title.
TX819.AIR68   1996
641.8'14--dc20   96-20167
                                                                   CIP

Printed and bound in Singapore

TITLE PAGE:
ROAST DUCK WITH PEACH SAUCE

Contents

About Sauces

In my imagination, I have always envisaged the craft of cooking and all its disciplines as an ancient, vigorous, and sprouting genealogical tree, whose main branches draw their life-giving sustenance from the sap in the trunk. From there, innumerable roots emanate, one of the oldest and most important, dating from time immemorial, being that of sauces.

The great sauces

The great classics have been around for centuries. Noble, powerful, aristocratic, and elegant, they form part of our heritage. These are sauces fit for feast days and special occasions.

The lesser sauces

There are multitudes of these, suitable for any occasion and every day. They can be prepared in a matter of moments, with very little effort, to complement a piece of meat or fish or a dish of pasta.

Modern sauces

These are the newcomers, quick and easy to prepare. They are very light, with fewer calories, and are kind to the digestion. They are particularly appropriate for salads, *crudités*, vegetables, and desserts.

The basic elements

All sauces, however simple or complex, should be based on good-quality ingredients. Aromatics, fresh herbs, spices, wines, alcohol, stocks, and *fumets* – all must be chosen with the utmost care.

The bartender

A sauce-maker is like a bartender mixing cocktails. It is vital to get the proportions right. Ingredients with a very strong flavor, like certain pungent spices, herbs, and alcohol, should be used in moderation.

The cook as alchemist

A pinch of this, a pinch of that – the creative process is bewitching. A flame licks up from the pan containing the bubbling, steaming potion, illuminating the sagacious face of the "saucerer." He inhales the fumes laden with the first aromas. His imagination is fired as he conjures up the magic of his sauce.

My sauces

From the age of fourteen, during my apprenticeship to a *pâtissier,* followed by many years in professional kitchens, I learned the secret of sauces, from the chefs with whom I worked. Later, I developed them to suit my own palate and created original new sauces to complement my dishes.

There are sauces to suit every season, every taste, every occasion, and the time available for their preparation. My objective when making a sauce, be it savory or sweet, is to provide the perfect accompaniment to a dish and to elevate it to gastronomic perfection – but never to dominate it.

In the course of a year at The Waterside Inn, I prepare hundreds of different sauces – modern, classic, light, or unctuous, depending on the dishes they are to accompany. Those in this book are among my favorites. They are creative and diverse, enormously enjoyable, and perfectly accessible to the home cook.

Cooking a sauce intoxicates the senses of smell, taste, and sight. The visual and odiferous pleasures it offers in its final cooking stages will tempt you to dream and discover the wonderful world of sauces.

The photographs

The exceptional technical quality of the photography allows me to guide you through every process of sauce-making, vividly bringing to life the crucial stages. Together, we shall develop your talents as a sauce-maker.

Practical Advice

Choosing and flavoring sauces

MENU PLANNING: Serve only one "grand" sauce at a meal and keep the others light and simple.

Do not serve a powerful, full-bodied sauce at the beginning of a meal.

Try to avoid serving sauces of the same color and texture, or with a similar base, such as wine or liqueurs. Do not make all the sauces at the same meal too classic or too modern. Your guests will appreciate a judicious balance.

SEASONAL PRODUCE: In the same way that you would choose the finest seasonal ingredients for a finished dish, make your sauces with the best seasonal produce. The end result will be full of flavor and all the more delicious.

SEASONING: Never add too much salt to a sauce before it has reached the desired consistency and taste. Add pepper only just before serving to retain its flavor and zip.

CURRY POWDER: Add a pinch of curry powder to foaming melted butter to enhance the flavors of steamed fish, white meats, and vegetables.

GARLIC: Always halve garlic cloves lengthwise and remove the green shoot, which can be indigestible.

MUSHROOMS: Their wild, musky aroma of forest bark and damp earth adds a special something to many sauces. It is better to wipe fresh mushrooms clean than to wash them, because they absorb water and lose their flavor. Chop or finely slice them and add to the sauce during cooking. Some varieties, such as common mushrooms, tend to lack flavor, so be generous with these. Others, such as shiitake, have quite an aggressive flavor and should be used sparingly. Dried mushrooms are a good substitute for fresh

TO CRUSH GARLIC, PUT THE PEELED CLOVES IN A MORTAR WITH A LARGE PINCH OF COARSE SALT

CRUSH THE GARLIC TO A PASTE WITH A PESTLE

(soak them first). For the ultimate pleasure, black or white truffles can be added to numerous sauces a few minutes before serving.

SAFFRON: To obtain the maximum flavor when using saffron threads, pound them in a mortar or crush them with your fingertips into the palm of your hand, then infuse them in a little warm water.

SHELLFISH COOKING JUICES: Keep the cooking juices from oysters, mussels, clams, etc. As soon as possible after cooking the mollusks, add a small amount to fish sauces to reinforce their flavor and make them more complex.

SHALLOTS: Shallots become bitter after chopping, so rinse them under cold water before using in a sauce.

VEGETABLE ESSENCES: These are used to lighten a sauce that is over-rich, powerful, or too thick, or to add a more aromatic flavor to a sauce or vegetable *court-bouillon*. They can also be served separately in a ramekin to accompany steamed fish, or stirred warm into a vinaigrette to serve with vegetables or shellfish.

Vegetable essences can be made with almost any kind of vegetables. Chop them finely or coarsely, depending on their structure, and place in a pan with a very small amount of liquid (water or chicken stock). Cover and cook until tender, then strain the essence through a fine-mesh conical sieve and keep in a small airtight jar.

VINEGAR AND LEMON: A few drops of vinegar or lemon juice added to a characterless sauce just before serving will pep up the taste.

Preparing, keeping, and freezing sauces

PREPARATION TIME: The preparation times given in this book are based on ingredients that have already been measured and prepared as indicated in the ingredients list. They do not include the time taken to peel, chop, slice, or blanch vegetables or bones, soften butter, etc, or any cooling time.

COOKING TIMES: The timings given for cooking and reducing sauces are intended only as guidelines, since the degree of heat will vary depending on your stove and the type of saucepan used. The only infallible way to ensure that a sauce has reached the desired consistency is to check it on the back of a spoon.

DEGREASING: The easiest way to degrease a stock is to let it cool completely at room temperature, then refrigerate it. The fat will solidify on the surface and can be carefully lifted off with a large spoon.

DEGLAZING: Liquid such as wine or stock is heated with the cooking juices and sediment left in the pan after roasting or pan-frying to make a sauce or gravy. Remove most of the fat and grease from the pan before adding the liquid.

STRAINING: Thin sauces can be passed straight through a conical sieve. Thicker sauces should be pushed through the sieve by pressing with the back of a ladle or twisting a small whisk.

HOT EMULSION SAUCES: These sauces do not like to be kept waiting. To enjoy them at their delicate best, make them at the last possible moment and serve immediately.

KEEPING SAUCES WARM: A *bain-marie* is best for this. Use a saucepan large enough to hold the pan or bowl containing the sauce, and fill the pan with hot water.

Dot flakes of butter over the surface of white sauces to prevent a skin from forming. Sauces that need a liaison or "smoothing" with butter should be kept in the *bain-marie*, and the liaison or butter added at the moment of serving.

FREEZING: All stocks and *fumets* freeze well. Store them in small, airtight freezer containers. Then, whenever you need some, just tip the frozen block of stock into a saucepan and heat gently.

A CLASSIC BOUQUET GARNI
CONSISTS OF A SPRIG OF
THYME, A BAY LEAF,
PARSLEY STEMS, AND A
LEEK LEAF

WRAP THE HERBS IN THE
LEEK LEAF AND TIE UP
THE BOUQUET GARNI
WITH STRING

Herbs and spices

This subject deserves an entire encyclopedia to do it justice instead of just a few lines. But since this is a book about sauces, I shall mention only those herbs and spices that are familiar to me and which I use to flavor and enhance my own cooking.

In Bray, I have created an herb garden on the banks of the Thames. Every day in the summer months, I painstakingly and parsimoniously pick the numerous different herbs I need for my sauces and salads. Freshness is a vital factor in the success of a sauce, and my herb garden is my trump card.

If you use dried herbs, keep them in airtight jars in a cool, dark place. Spices lose their color and flavor if they are kept too long; you should throw away any open jars after 3 – 6 months because the spice will add nothing to your sauces, and may even spoil them.

The golden rules for using herbs and spices are:
* Small quantities but good quality.
* Do not mix contradictory and powerful flavors.
If you obey these rules, you will discover a wonderful world of flavors – subtle, complex, musky, fresh, spicy, and delectable.

Fines herbes are a mixture of fresh herbs in equal quantities: chervil, chives, parsley, and tarragon. They should be snipped, not chopped, preferably only a short time before using so that they retain the maximum flavor and do not become bitter.

The most popular culinary herbs are: basil, bay leaf, chervil, chives, cilantro, dill, fennel, garlic, horseradish, lavender, lemon grass, lemon verbena, lovage, marjoram, mint, oregano, flat or curly parsley, rosemary, sage, savory, sorrel, tarragon, and thyme.

The most popular spices are: caraway, cardamom, cayenne, cinnamon, cloves, coriander seeds, cumin, curry, five-spice, ginger, juniper, mace, nutmeg, peppercorns (black, green, white, and pink), paprika, pimento, poppy seeds, saffron, and star anise.

Capers are also a popular ingredient, as is vanilla, the most famous of all aromatics for sweet sauces.

TO FLAVOR A SAUCE
WITH PEPPERCORNS,
CRUSH THEM AND
PLACE ON A PIECE OF
CHEESECLOTH

FOLD UP THE EDGES
TO MAKE A PURSE
AND TIE WITH
STRING

Dairy products

These play an extremely important part in sauce-making.

UNSALTED BUTTER: The finest of all dairy products. It is natural and healthy and practically indispensable in the kitchen. Its delicate taste and different complexities vary according to its provenance and origins. It adds the finishing touch to many of my sauces, but I always use it in moderation. I use only unsalted butter in my cooking. This is essential for making clarified butter and desirable for all sauces.

At The Waterside Inn, after many blind tastings, the butter I have chosen for the table and for my *beurres blancs* and sauces is the *appellation contrôlée* Echiré from the Deux-Sèvres. Its quality and value place it among the very best French butters.

When either unsalted and salted butter is melted, its components separate into 15 – 20% water, 4% protein, and the balance butterfat.

HEAVY CREAM: This tolerates heat extremely well during cooking and can even be reduced by boiling. It is often used as a liaison, but above all it makes sauces creamy and velvety.

CRÈME FRAÎCHE: This can be heated to not more than 175°F, after which it will separate. To use it in a hot sauce, whisk it into the sauce off the heat, without further cooking. This slightly acidulated cream is light and refreshing and is delicious added to most cold sauces.

FROMAGE BLANC: This soft, unripened cheese is the champion of low-calorie sauces. One type, called Quark, is available in both lowfat and nonfat versions. It is perfect for summer sauces, but its neutral taste demands the addition of spices, herbs, etc.

YOGURT: I use tiny quantities of yogurt to finish certain fish sauces in order to add a touch of acidity. I use it more often in low-calorie summer vinaigrettes and in some fruit coulis, where it develops a hint of acidity and freshness.

HARD CHEESES: The most important and best are Parmesan, Gruyère, Emmenthal, and Cheddar. I always buy medium-aged farmhouse cheeses, which have a full, sublime flavor. These cheeses are usually used freshly grated to finish a sauce. It takes a few minutes after they have been added for their savor to develop, so you should use them judiciously and parsimoniously at first, checking their development before adding more to the sauce.

Do not use cheap, poor-quality cheese, which can ruin a sauce by tasting rancid, soapy, or too salty.

ROQUEFORT: My noble Lord Roquefort will acquire star status in a salad dressing, a cold sauce for *crudités,* and certain hot sauces. I adore Roquefort. Used in moderation, it creates an explosion of different savors in a sauce. Bleu d'Auvergne and Fourme d'Ambert make adequate substitutes, but cannot equal the real thing.

Sauce-making equipment

ALL YOU NEED TO MAKE PERFECT SAUCES

OPPOSITE PAGE:

1. SAUCEPAN WITH SLOPING SIDES,
   SAUCEPAN, STOCKPOT
2. STRAIGHT-SIDED SAUCEPANS, BAIN-MARIE
   (DOUBLE BOILER)
3. LARGE SPOON, LADLE, SKIMMER, SLOTTED
   SPOON, FINE STRAINER
4. KITCHEN SCALES, MEASURING CUP,
   COOKING THERMOMETER
5. MORTAR AND PESTLE
6. STRAINER, WIRE-MESH AND RIGID
   CONICAL SIEVES
7. BLENDER GOBLET, HAND-HELD BLENDER
8. ZESTER, MANDOLINE
9. ASSORTED BOWLS

THIS PAGE, LEFT TO RIGHT:

BALLOON WHISK
RUBBER AND WOODEN SPATULAS,
    WOODEN SPOON
WOODEN POUNDER, DRUM SIEVE

All this equipment can be obtained from M.O.R.A.
(Matérial Outillage Rationnel pour l'Alimentation)
13 rue Montmartre, 75001 Paris, France.
Tel: 45 08 19 24
Fax: 45 08 49 05

These are indispensable to the preparation of the great classic sauces and play a significant part in many others. Given their importance, they should be prepared with great care.

Stocks are the very foundation of sauces; on their quality depends the success of your sauces and your mastery of sauce-making.

Stocks

THE GOLDEN RULES OF STOCK-MAKING

* All the ingredients — meat, poultry, or fish bones, aromatics, vegetables, wines, etc. — must be extremely fresh and of the highest quality.

* Equally important: do not drown the stock at the outset by adding too much water to the ingredients; it will make it tasteless and watery. Better to add too little water than too much; if necessary you can always add more cold water during cooking.

* Always add cold water to a stock. Hot water will make it cloudy and you will lose the desired crystal clarity.

* Cooking a stock longer does not make it better — quite the reverse. Long cooking can actually be detrimental, since the stock becomes heavy and loses its flavor. Follow the cooking times in the recipes precisely; only veal stock needs several hours' cooking.

* For a double depth of flavor, cook the stock twice, using cold water the first time, and the cooled batch of stock the second time.

In essence, stocks are embryonic sauces, which must be carefully nurtured and titivated. They should be cooked at a simmer and never allowed to boil, and must be skimmed and degreased at regular intervals to remove all impurities. Finally, they must be strained gently and delicately through a wire-mesh conical sieve, taking care not to cloud their clarity.

Veal Stock

Fond de veau

PUT THE BONES IN THE
ROASTING PAN

*Veal stock forms the base for almost all brown sauces, and is
often used in fish sauces as well.*

Makes 1 quart
PREPARATION TIME: 30 MINUTES
COOKING TIME: ABOUT 3 HOURS

Ingredients:
$3^1/4$ POUNDS VEAL BONES, CHOPPED
$1/2$ CALF'S FOOT, SPLIT LENGTHWISE, CHOPPED, AND
BLANCHED
2 CARROTS, CUT IN ROUNDS
$2/3$ CUP COARSELY CHOPPED ONION
1 CUP DRY WHITE WINE
1 CELERY STALK, THINLY SLICED
6 TOMATOES, PEELED, SEEDED, AND CHOPPED
2 CUPS THINLY SLICED BUTTON MUSHROOMS
2 GARLIC CLOVES
1 BOUQUET GARNI (PAGE 10), INCLUDING A
SPRIG OF TARRAGON

RIGHT: ADD THE
VEGETABLES AND
AROMATICS

INSET: STRAIN THE
STOCK AND COOL IT
OVER A BOWL OF ICE

BROWN THE BONES,
CARROTS, AND ONIONS

Preheat the oven to 425°F. Put the veal bones and calf's
foot in a roasting pan and brown in the oven, turning
them from time to time with a slotted spoon. When they
have browned, add the carrots and onion, mix together,
and cook for 5 minutes longer. Using the slotted spoon,
transfer all the contents of the roasting pan to a large
saucepan or casserole. Pour off the fat from the roasting
pan and deglaze with the white wine, scraping up all the
sediment. Set over high heat and reduce by half, then
pour the wine into the saucepan. Add 3 quarts cold
water and bring to a boil over high heat. As soon as the
liquid boils, reduce the heat so that the surface is barely
trembling. Simmer for 10 minutes, then skim well and
add all the other ingredients.

Simmer the stock, uncovered, for $2^1/2$ hours,
skimming as necessary. Strain through a fine-mesh
conical sieve into a bowl and cool over ice (see page 22).

DEMI-GLACE OR GLACE: Reduce the strained
stock by one-third to make a *demi-glace*; reduce by half for
a *glace*. These *glaces* enhance sauces, adding moistness and
a fuller flavor. But they cannot add finesse and subtlety,
since the lengthy cooking time involved destroys some of
their delicate flavor and aroma.

DEGLAZE THE PAN WITH
THE WINE

SKIM THE SURFACE OF
THE STOCK

Chicken Stock

Fond de volaille

I sometimes add half a veal shank, when preparing this stock, which makes it extra rich and unctuous.

Makes about 1 1/2 quarts
PREPARATION TIME: 15 MINUTES
COOKING TIME: ABOUT 1 3/4 HOURS

Ingredients:
1 STEWING CHICKEN, WEIGHING 3 1/4 POUNDS, OR AN
EQUAL WEIGHT OF CHICKEN CARCASSES OR WINGS,
BLANCHED AND REFRESHED
2 CARROTS, CUT IN CHUNKS
WHITE PART OF 2 LEEKS, CUT IN CHUNKS
1 CELERY STALK, COARSELY CHOPPED
1 ONION, STUDDED WITH 2 CLOVES
2 CUPS THINLY SLICED BUTTON MUSHROOMS
1 BOUQUET GARNI (PAGE 10)

Put the chicken or carcasses in a saucepan and cover with 2 1/2 quarts cold water. Bring to a boil over high heat, then immediately lower the heat and keep at a simmer. After 5 minutes, skim the surface and add all the other ingredients. Cook gently for 1 1/2 hours, without boiling, skimming whenever necessary.

Strain the stock through a wire-mesh conical sieve and cool it as quickly as possible (see page 22).

Lamb Stock

Fond d'agneau

This lamb stock is light in both flavor and appearance. I use it for deglazing in many roasted or pan-fried lamb recipes, such as a navarin. It can form the basis for a sauce, in which case I would flavor it with curry, star anise, mint, or saffron, etc to complement the dish. For a wonderful taste of spring, I sometimes use the stock to moisten a couscous garnished with tender young vegetables.

Makes 1 quart
PREPARATION TIME: 30 MINUTES
COOKING TIME: ABOUT 2 HOURS

Ingredients:
3 1/4 POUNDS NECK OR SHOULDER OF LAMB, SKIN AND
FAT REMOVED, CUT IN PIECES
2 SMALL CARROTS, CUT IN ROUNDS
2/3 CUP COARSELY CHOPPED ONION
1 CUP DRY WHITE WINE
4 TOMATOES, PEELED, SEEDED, AND CHOPPED
2 GARLIC CLOVES
1 BOUQUET GARNI (PAGE 10), INCLUDING 2 SPRIGS
OF TARRAGON AND A CELERY STALK
6 WHITE PEPPERCORNS, CRUSHED

Preheat the oven to 425°F. Put the pieces of lamb in a roasting pan and brown in the hot oven, turning them over from time to time with a slotted spoon. When the lamb has colored, add the carrots and onions, mix together, and cook for 5 minutes longer. Still using the slotted spoon, transfer all the contents of the roasting pan to a large saucepan or casserole. Pour off the fat from the roasting pan, deglaze with the white wine, and reduce by half. Pour the reduced wine into the saucepan, add 2 1/2 quarts cold water, and bring to a boil over high heat. As soon as the liquid boils, reduce the heat so that the surface is barely trembling. Simmer for 10 minutes, then skim the surface and add all the other ingredients.

Simmer, uncovered, for 1 1/2 hours, skimming the surface as necessary. Strain the stock through a fine-mesh conical sieve into a bowl and cool it as quickly as possible (see page 22).

Game Stock

Fond de gibier

This stock makes the perfect sauce for pan-fried noisettes of venison. Deglaze the pan with port wine, add a teaspoon of red-currant jelly, and then add the game stock. Whisk in a small piece of butter and season to taste. Delicious!

Makes 1¹/₂ quarts
PREPARATION TIME: 30 MINUTES
COOKING TIME: 2¹/₄ HOURS

Ingredients:
3 TABLESPOONS PEANUT OIL
4 POUNDS GAME TRIMMINGS, CARCASSES, NECKS,
WINGS, ETC, CUT IN PIECES
2 SMALL CARROTS, CUT IN ROUNDS
I CUP COARSELY CHOPPED ONIONS
¹/₂ HEAD OF GARLIC, HALVED WIDTHWISE
2 CUPS RED WINE (PREFERABLY CÔTES DU RHÔNE)
2 CUPS VEAL STOCK (PAGE 16)
8 JUNIPER BERRIES, CRUSHED
8 CORIANDER SEEDS, CRUSHED
I BOUQUET GARNI (PAGE 10), INCLUDING 2 SAGE
LEAVES AND A CELERY STALK

Preheat the oven to 425°F. Heat the oil in a roasting pan, then put in the game carcasses or trimmings and brown in the hot oven, turning them from time to time with a slotted spoon. When the meat has browned, add the carrots, onions, and garlic, mix together, and cook for 5 minutes longer. With the slotted spoon, transfer all the contents of the roasting pan to a large saucepan or casserole. Pour off the fat from the roasting pan and deglaze with the red wine. Set over high heat and reduce the wine by half, then pour it into the saucepan. Add 2 quarts cold water and bring to a boil over high heat. As soon as the liquid boils, reduce the heat so that the surface barely trembles. Simmer for 10 minutes, then skim well and add all the other ingredients.

Simmer the stock, uncovered, for 2 hours, skimming the surface as necessary. Strain it through a fine-mesh conical sieve into a bowl and cool as quickly as possible (see page 22).

Once the stock has been strained, you can reduce it by one-third to give it more body. Like all stocks, it will keep well for several days in the refrigerator, or for three or four months in the freezer.

Fish
Stock or Fumet

Fumet de poisson

Fish stock can be used as the base for an aspic to serve with cold fish. Just add a little unflavored gelatin and season with salt and pepper before the gelatin sets. If you intend to use the stock for a red wine sauce, substitute red wine for the white when making the stock.

Makes 2 quarts
PREPARATION TIME: 20 MINUTES
COOKING TIME: ABOUT 30 MINUTES

Ingredients:
$3^1/4$ POUNDS BONES AND TRIMMINGS OF WHITE FISH
(E.G. SOLE, TURBOT, WHITING), CUT IN PIECES
4 TABLESPOONS BUTTER
WHITE OF 2 LEEKS, THINLY SLICED
$^1/2$ CUP THINLY SLICED ONION
I CUP THINLY SLICED BUTTON MUSHROOMS
I CUP DRY WHITE WINE
I BOUQUET GARNI (PAGE I0)
2 SLICES OF LEMON
8 WHITE PEPPERCORNS, CRUSHED AND WRAPPED IN A
PIECE OF CHEESECLOTH (PAGE II)

Rinse the fish bones and trimmings under cold running water, then drain (I). In a saucepan, melt the butter and sweat the vegetables over low heat for a few minutes. Add the fish bones and trimmings (2), bubble gently for a few moments, and then pour in the wine (3). Cook until it has evaporated by two-thirds, then add $2^1/2$ quarts cold water (4). Bring to a boil, lower the heat, skim the surface, and add the bouquet garni and lemon. Simmer very gently for 25 minutes, skimming as necessary. I0 minutes before the end of cooking, add the cheesecloth-wrapped peppercorns.

Gently ladle the stock through a fine-mesh conical sieve and cool it as quickly as possible (see page 22).

FISH VELOUTÉ: For an excellent fish *velouté*, add $^1/4$ cup white roux (page 33) per quart of stock and cook for 20 minutes.

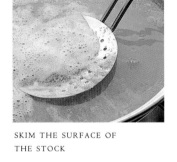

SKIM THE SURFACE OF
THE STOCK

ADD THE CHEESECLOTH-
WRAPPED PEPPERCORNS

STRAIN THE STOCK
THROUGH A FINE-MESH
CONICAL SIEVE

Vegetable Stock or Nage

Court-bouillon de légumes ou Nage

Nages are light, aromatic poaching stocks, and I like to add a hint of acidity to mine, hence the vinegar. I don't, however, use vinegar in my classic vegetable stock. You can substitute or add your own choice of seasonal vegetables, varying the stock with nice ripe tomatoes in summer, a few wild mushrooms in the fall (chanterelles add a particularly fine aroma), and so on.

Makes 1½ quarts
PREPARATION TIME: 15 MINUTES
COOKING TIME: 45 MINUTES

Ingredients:
3 CARROTS, CUT IN ROUNDS
WHITE PART OF 2 LEEKS, THINLY SLICED
2 CELERY STALKS, THINLY SLICED
½ CUP VERY THINLY SLICED BULB FENNEL
1 HEAPED CUP THINLY SLICED SHALLOTS
⅔ CUP THINLY SLICED ONION
2 UNPEELED GARLIC CLOVES
1 BOUQUET GARNI (PAGE 10)
1 CUP DRY WHITE WINE
2 QUARTS WATER
3 TABLESPOONS WHITE WINE VINEGAR (ONLY FOR A *NAGE*)
10 WHITE PEPPERCORNS, CRUSHED AND WRAPPED
IN CHEESECLOTH (PAGE 11)

Put all the ingredients except the peppercorns in a saucepan. Bring to a boil over high heat, then cook at a bare simmer for 45 minutes, skimming as necessary. After 35 minutes, add the cheesecloth-wrapped peppercorns. Strain through a fine-mesh conical sieve into a bowl and cool as quickly as possible (see below).

COOLING AND FREEZING STOCKS

In the restaurant I cool my strained stocks very rapidly using a blast freezer to prevent the spread of bacteria. At home, I fill a container with ice cubes and plunge in the pan or bowl of boiling stock, which cools quite quickly. As soon as it is cold, I transfer it to airtight containers, keeping what I need in the refrigerator and freezing the rest. All stocks can be refrigerated several days, or kept several weeks in the freezer.

PUT THE INGREDIENTS
INTO THE SAUCEPAN

SKIM THE SURFACE OF
THE STOCK

RIGHT: STRAIN THE STOCK
AND COOL IT QUICKLY
OVER A BOWL OF ICE

Cooked Marinade

Marinade ordinaire cuite

Large pieces of meat or game can be left in the cold marinade for one to three days; smaller pieces should be marinated for one or two hours. If you plan to serve the meat the same day, it can be placed in the marinade while this is still warm. Always use tongs or a fork to turn the meat in the marinade, never your fingers, which will spoil it.

The addition of a small amount of marinade to a game sauce will reinforce its structure and flavor.

Makes 1 1/2 quarts
(Sufficient for a large piece of meat)
PREPARATION TIME: ABOUT 10 MINUTES
COOKING TIME: ABOUT 25 MINUTES

Ingredients:
1 1/2 TABLESPOONS BUTTER
2 CARROTS, CUT IN ROUNDS
2 ONIONS, ROUGHLY CHOPPED
1 CELERY STALK, THINLY SLICED
1 QUART RED WINE (PREFERABLY CÔTES DU RHÔNE)
7 TABLESPOONS RED WINE VINEGAR
3 CUPS WATER
1 BOUQUET GARNI (PAGE 10), INCLUDING A SPRIG
OF ROSEMARY
1/2 HEAD OF GARLIC, HALVED WIDTHWISE
2 CLOVES
A PINCH OF CRUSHED PEPPERCORNS

In a saucepan, melt the butter and sweat the vegetables for a few minutes. Add all the other ingredients and bring to a boil over high heat. Immediately lower the heat and cook gently for 20 minutes, skimming the surface whenever necessary. Unless you are going to serve the meat the same day, cool the marinade completely before using it.

C H A P T E R   2

The choice of a liaison depends entirely on personal taste and the time available to make the sauce. It is like the gradation between a steak cooked very rare and one that is very well done; the range in between is enormous.

In this chapter, my purpose is to guide you through the different methods and types of liaison, explaining how to use them and which method best suits which type of sauce — but there are no rigid rules.

L i a i s o n s   &

I n s t a n t   S a u c e s

Although very thick sauces are no longer fashionable, there is no need to go too far in the other direction; any excess is ridiculous. We have all suffered ultra-light offerings from contemporary chefs, which are more like badly seasoned bouillons *than sauces. They remind me of the days of nouvelle cuisine, when you needed a magnifying glass to find the chef's minuscule creation on a huge plate. A sauce is not a glass of water; its consistency is as important as its taste, and it is vital to strike a happy balance.*

The popularity of the sauce spoon spread in the 1960s and enabled us easily and elegantly to sup up and enjoy the more liquid, lighter, foamy sauces that are better suited to today's tastes.

It is worth mentioning the very simplest liaisons, which require no recipe, such as a few caramelized onions, crushed into a sauce with a fork, or a little roasted carrot or potato given the same treatment. Garlic or shallots baked in their skins on a bed of coarse salt make a lovely thickener for lamb gravy or sauce from a pot-roasted chicken.

Also included in this chapter are some very quick recipes that require virtually no cooking. You could devise many others using the same simple principles.

THICKENING AND LIGHTENING
A SAUCE WITH BUTTER

Liaison techniques

Bread Crumbs

Bread crumbs are used as a thickening agent for rustic, flavorful sauces. In country cooking, they are used to thicken the broth from a pot-au-feu or the pan juices from a roast. These are my favorite sauces when I cook at my house in Gassin in Provence.

FRESH BREAD CRUMBS:

Crumble them into the warm sauce and cook very gently for about 20 minutes, whisking from time to time. When the sauce reaches the desired consistency, serve it just as it is, or pass it through a fine conical strainer.

TOASTED BREAD CRUMBS:

Crumble them into a bowl, and drizzle in a little olive oil plus, if desired, a small quantity of ground almonds. Mix thoroughly with a fork. Add the mixture to your warm sauce and bring to a boil over low heat. Bubble gently for 5-10 minutes until the sauce has thickened.

Egg yolks

Sauces bound with egg yolks have a velvety texture and delicate color. They always remind me of the creamy blanquette de veau that my mother prepared at home when I was a child.

In a bowl, break up the egg yolks with a very little barely tepid liquid: use milk, wine, chicken stock, etc. depending on the sauce. Off the heat, pour the yolks into the almost boiling sauce, stirring with a wooden spoon. Over low heat, reheat the sauce, stirring constantly, until it lightly coats the back of the spoon. It is essential not to let the sauce boil, or it will separate. As soon as it has thickened, pass it through a fine conical strainer into a clean saucepan and keep warm.

Cornstarch, rice flour, and arrowroot

These vegetable thickeners are quick and easy to use, need no special skill, and are ideal when you need a sauce in a hurry.

In a bowl, dissolve the thickening agent in a little cold liquid — water, milk, or wine — and pour into the boiling sauce. Simmer for about 10 minutes; the sauce will thicken almost instantaneously.

Heavy cream

Cream-thickened sauces are often used for fish, poultry, veloutés, and certain soups. They add a velvet-smooth quality, which I love.

Always use heavy cream. You will need about 10-20% cream in proportion to the quantity of sauce. Boil the cream for a few minutes, then stir it into the boiling sauce.

The consistency, taste, and properties of heavy cream vary from country to country. For example, in the U.S., it is soft and delicate and can be stirred directly into the sauce and boiled without separating. In France, crème fraîche is slightly acidulated and cannot easily be added uncooked to a sauce, or it will split.

SWIRL THE BUTTER INTO A SAUCE, A LITTLE
AT A TIME, TO LIGHTEN AND THICKEN IT

Blood

Blood is mainly used as a thickener for sauces for game, such as venison and wild boar, or in the sauce for canard au sang. I use a touch in the red wine sauce that I often serve with duck at The Waterside Inn, and also in civet of hare, which is a favorite dish of mine.

Blood used for cooking almost always comes from pork, rabbit, or poultry (usually chicken). It is important that it does not coagulate; a few drops of vinegar added as soon as you obtain the blood will prevent this.

Allow about $2/3$ cup blood for 1 quart of sauce, or a little more if you want a thicker sauce.

Take the almost boiling sauce off the heat and add the blood, stirring continuously with a wooden spatula. Replace the pan over medium heat and cook the sauce until it thickens, stirring all the time. As soon as the surface begins to tremble, stop the cooking and immediately pass the sauce through a fine conical strainer into another pan. Keep it warm and serve it as soon as possible.

Lightening and thickening with butter

Incorporating butter into a sauce improves it in five important ways, making it lighter, smoother, glossier, thicker, and mellower. Once ready, these delicate sauces must not be allowed to boil and should be served as soon as possible.

The butter should be well-chilled, almost frozen. Take the boiling sauce off the heat and incorporate small pieces of butter (about 1 teaspoon), one at a time. Either use a balloon whisk or hold the pan handle firmly and swirl or shake the pan from side to side, until all the butter is incorporated.

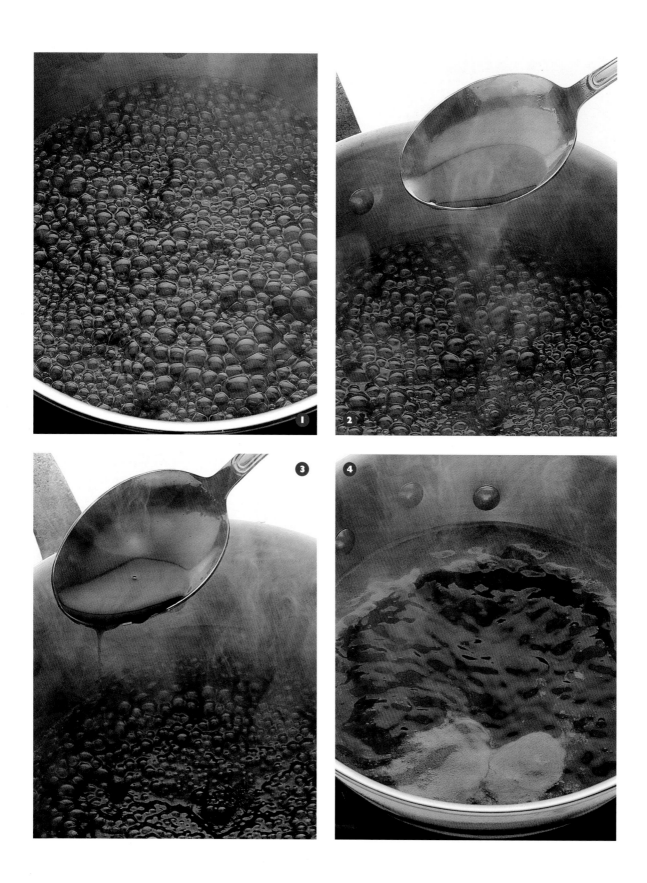

Reduction

You should be able to judge by eye when a sauce has reached the desired consistency by reduction, but it is helpful to use the back of a spoon to gauge the precise thickness. Let the sauce cool slightly before running your finger down the spoon.

Reduce the sauce over high heat to obtain the required consistency — a light juice (1), slightly syrupy (2), syrupy (3), or the very thick, rich demi-glace (6). As the sauce reduces, impurities rise to the surface (4); skim off as necessary (5). Never season a reduction sauce before it reaches the desired consistency.

Using a blender

Sauces emulsified in a blender are very light and should be used immediately to retain their airy quality. They are often based on vegetable or fish stock, or beurre blanc.

Pour the finished sauce into the goblet of a blender, or use a hand blender, and whizz for 2–5 minutes, depending on how airy and mousse-like you want your sauce to be.

Beurre manié

Beurre manié, or kneaded butter, is used to thicken sauces rapidly. Use only a small quantity, or the sauce will become too heavy.

It usually consists of equal parts softened butter and flour, mashed together (uncooked) with a fork. Using a small whisk, incorporate small quantities of beurre manié into the sauce over high heat. The sauce will thicken immediately. Let it bubble a few times, then as soon as it reaches the desired consistency, pass it through a wire-mesh conical strainer.

Clarified butter

Clarified butter is used to cook meat over a high heat because it does not burn and blacken as unclarified butter would. It is also used for emulsified sauces like hollandaise and its derivatives and for making brown roux. During the clarifying process, the butter loses about 20% of its original weight.

To make about ¹/₂ cup clarified butter, start with 10 tablespoons unsalted butter. Melt this over a very gentle heat and bring slowly to a boil. Skim off the froth from the surface. Carefully pour the liquid butter into a bowl, taking care not to include any of the milky sediment from the bottom of the pan. The clarified butter should be the color of a light olive oil.

Clarified butter will keep in the refrigerator for several weeks.

SAUCES WILL FROTH UP
WHEN EMULSIFIED
WITH A HAND BLENDER,
SO MAKE SURE YOU USE
A DEEP ENOUGH
SAUCEPAN

SKIM OFF THE FROTH
FROM THE SURFACE OF
THE BUTTER

CAREFULLY POUR THE
LIQUID CLARIFIED
BUTTER INTO A BOWL

White Roux

This roux is classically used as a thickener in all white sauces.

Makes just over ¹/₂ cup
PREPARATION TIME: 3 MINUTES
COOKING TIME: 4 MINUTES

Ingredients:
6 TABLESPOONS BUTTER
¹/₂ CUP FLOUR

Melt the butter in a heavy-based saucepan (1). Off the heat, add the flour (2) and stir in with a small whisk or a wooden spoon (3), then cook over medium heat for 3 minutes, stirring continuously (4). Transfer to a bowl, cover with plastic wrap, and keep at room temperature, or store in the refrigerator for several days.

Blond Roux

This pale roux is used to thicken veloutés *and sauces where a neutral color is required, particularly those for lamb, veal, and all poultry.*

Makes just over ¹/₂ cup
PREPARATION TIME: 3 MINUTES
COOKING TIME: 6 MINUTES

Ingredients:
6 TABLESPOONS BUTTER
¹/₂ CUP FLOUR

Melt the butter in a heavy-based saucepan. Take the pan off the heat and stir in the flour with a small whisk or a spatula. Cook the roux over medium heat for 5 minutes, stirring continuously, until it becomes a pale hazelnut-brown (5). Transfer to a bowl, cover with plastic wrap, and keep at room temperature. The roux can be stored in the refrigerator for several days.

Brown Roux

This roux is used to thicken many brown sauces. The clarified butter gives the sauce a deep color without adding any of the bitterness or unpleasant flavor of burned butter.

Makes just over ¹/₂ cup
PREPARATION TIME: 3 MINUTES
COOKING TIME: 9 MINUTES

Ingredients:
6 TABLESPOONS CLARIFIED BUTTER (PAGE 31)
¹/₂ CUP FLOUR

Heat the clarified butter in a heavy-based saucepan (6). Take the pan off the heat and stir in the flour using a small whisk or a spatula. Cook the roux over medium heat for 8 minutes, stirring continuously, until it becomes chestnut-brown (7). Transfer to a bowl, cover with plastic wrap, and keep at room temperature. The roux can be stored in the refrigerator for several days.

Fromage Blanc Sauce with Curry

Sauce au fromage blanc au parfum de curry

Use this sauce as a dressing for a summer salad of green beans, new potatoes, or crudités, or with cold cooked mussels.

You can adjust the quantity of curry slightly to suit your own taste, or even substitute 1/3 cup fresh mint, which you infuse in the milk. This version is delicious with cold pasta and a scattering of shredded mint leaves.

Serves 6
PREPARATION TIME: 3 MINUTES
COOKING TIME: 2 MINUTES

Ingredients:
1/2 CUP MILK
1 TABLESPOON CURRY POWDER
3/4 POUND (1 1/2 CUPS) FROMAGE BLANC (WHICHEVER FAT CONTENT YOU PREFER)
SALT AND FRESHLY GROUND PEPPER

In a small saucepan, bring the milk to a boil. Add the curry and simmer for 2 minutes, then leave at room temperature to cool completely. Strain the cold curry-flavored milk through a wire-mesh sieve, then stir it into the *fromage blanc*. Season to taste with salt and pepper. The sauce is now ready to use.

Yogurt Sauce

Sauce au yaourt

This refreshing sauce is excellent with all cold vegetables, cold pasta, fish, and hard-boiled eggs. It is very quick to make.

Serves 8
PREPARATION TIME: 10 MINUTES

Ingredients:
2 1/2 CUPS PLAIN YOGURT
1/2 CUP MAYONNAISE (SEE PAGE 109)
2 TABLESPOONS SNIPPED FRESH HERBS OF YOUR CHOICE (E.G. CHERVIL, PARSLEY, CHIVES, TARRAGON)
1 MEDIUM TOMATO, PEELED, SEEDED, AND DICED
A SMALL PINCH OF CAYENNE, OR 4 DROPS OF HOT-PEPPER SAUCE
SALT

Mix all the ingredients together and, *voilà*, your sauce is ready to serve.

Herb Butter Sauce

Beurre battu aux herbes

At The Waterside Inn, I roll boiled potatoes or small carrots in this sauce to make them savory and shiny.

Serves 6
PREPARATION TIME: 3 MINUTES
COOKING TIME: 5 MINUTES

Ingredients:
1/2 CUP COLD WATER
A SMALL BUNCH OF EQUAL QUANTITIES OF TARRAGON AND FLAT-LEAF PARSLEY, CHOPPED
14 TABLESPOONS BUTTER, CHILLED AND DICED
JUICE OF 1/2 LEMON
SALT AND FRESHLY GROUND PEPPER

Put the water and herbs in a saucepan and bring to a boil. Over very low heat, add the butter, whisking continuously. At the last moment, add the lemon juice, season to taste with salt and pepper, and pass the sauce through a wire-mesh sieve. Serve immediately.

Fishbone Sauce

Sauce à l'arête

This sauce is quick to prepare, light, and full of flavor. It goes very well with poached fish or steamed scallops.

Serves 4
PREPARATION TIME: 10 MINUTES
COOKING TIME: 10 MINUTES

Ingredients:
10 TABLESPOONS BUTTER, DICED
1/3 CUP CHOPPED SHALLOT
1/2 POUND WHITE FISH BONES (E.G. SOLE OR
TURBOT), ROUGHLY CHOPPED
1/2 CUP DRY WHITE WINE
1/2 CUP COLD WATER
1 SPRIG OF THYME
A FEW DROPS OF LEMON JUICE
SALT AND FRESHLY GROUND PEPPER

Melt 4 tablespoons butter in a small saucepan. Add the shallot and fish bones and sweat gently for 3 minutes, stirring with a wooden spoon. Pour in the wine and cook for 2 minutes. Add the water and thyme and bubble for 3 minutes, then skim the surface if necessary. Toss in the remaining butter, one piece at a time, rotating the pan and swirling it about to incorporate the butter, then add the lemon juice. Season to taste with salt and pepper, and pass the sauce through a wire-mesh conical sieve. It is ready to use.

Fresh Goat~Cheese Sauce with Rosemary

Sauce au fromage de chèvre frais et au romarin

Serve this sauce with a basket of crudités or cold dishes such as poached fish, roast or poached chicken, or with large pink shrimp.

Serves 6
PREPARATION TIME: 3 MINUTES

Ingredients:
1 CUP MILK (IF THE CHEESE HAS A VERY SOFT
CONSISTENCY, YOU MAY NEED ONLY 2/3 - 3/4 CUP)
1/4 CUP FRESH ROSEMARY NEEDLES
3/4 POUND FRESH GOAT CHEESE, SOFTENED WITH A
SPATULA
SALT AND FRESHLY GROUND PEPPER

In a small saucepan, bring the milk to a boil. Add the rosemary needles, cover the pan, and leave to infuse until completely cold. Strain the cooled milk, whisk it into the goat cheese, and season to taste with salt and pepper. The sauce is now ready to serve.

CHAPTER 3

Vinaigrettes are used to dress all kinds of salads, from tender green leaves to robust, crunchy vegetables. They are also used for hors d'oeuvres — crudités, composed salads made with thinly sliced raw or smoked fish, seafood, baby vegetables, asparagus tips, snow peas, and mushrooms. They even marry well with certain fruits, like citrus, apples, and raspberries.

Vinaigrettes, Flavored Oils & Vinegars

Summer is the best time for vinaigrettes, which pep up the appetite, particularly in very hot weather.

Take care never to combine conflicting colors and textures, and do not use too many ingredients which will detract from or spoil the fine flavor of the principal ingredient. By all means be creative, but keep your imagination under control.

Vinaigrettes are all the better for being prepared a few minutes in advance, as they will lose some of their savor and aroma if you make them too long before using them.

The judicious addition of a spoonful of chicken or veal stock, Américaine sauce, or a vegetable purée can transform a vinaigrette. Fresh snipped herbs or a touch of spice add the final aesthetic and gustatory note.

A GOOD VINAIGRETTE WILL
ADD LIFE TO ANY SALAD

VINEGARS: *The most commonly used vinegars are: red wine, white wine, sherry, balsamic, champagne (which is used for beurre blanc), fruit such as raspberry or black-currant (homemade is best), tarragon, cider, and garlic-flavored wine vinegar.*

I have included a recipe for fruit vinegar in this chapter. You do not need one for tarragon vinegar: simply immerse a few sprigs of tarragon in a bottle of white wine vinegar and leave it for several weeks to perfume and flavor the vinegar.

OILS: *The most popular oils are: olive, peanut, sunflower, corn, canola, hazelnut, walnut, sesame, grapeseed, and safflower. Some highly scented oils, like walnut or hazelnut, need to be diluted with a flavorless oil. Use one part flavored oil to two parts peanut oil. These oils and vinegars form the basis for every kind of vinaigrette, together with emulsifiers such as cream, yogurt, fromage blanc, mustard, and other refreshing condiments.*

Roquefort Vinaigrette

Vinaigrette au roquefort

I enjoy this dressing in winter served with bitter leaves like dandelion, frisée, or escarole. It is also good with crisply cooked green beans served warm and tossed in the vinaigrette just before serving.

Serves 6
PREPARATION TIME: 5 MINUTES

Ingredients:
3 TABLESPOONS WALNUT OIL
3 TABLESPOONS SAFFLOWER OR SUNFLOWER OIL
2 TABLESPOONS TARRAGON VINEGAR
2 OUNCES ROQUEFORT, CRUSHED WITH A FORK
1 TEASPOON SNIPPED TARRAGON LEAVES
A FEW DROPS OF WORCESTERSHIRE SAUCE
SALT AND FRESHLY GROUND PEPPER

Combine all the ingredients in a bowl and mix together with a small whisk.

Lavender Vinaigrette

Vinaigrette à la lavande

The flavors of lavender and honey subtly flavor this vinaigrette, which is excellent with raw sliced mushrooms or cucumber, or with tender salad leaves.

Serves 6
PREPARATION TIME: 5 MINUTES

Ingredients:
FLOWERS FROM A STEM OF NOT-TOO-FLOWERY
FRESH LAVENDER
3 TABLESPOONS PEANUT OIL
3 TABLESPOONS OLIVE OIL
2 TABLESPOONS WHITE WINE VINEGAR
1 TEASPOON HONEY
LEAVES FROM A SPRIG OF THYME
SALT AND FRESHLY GROUND PEPPER

Put all the ingredients in a blender and whizz for 30 seconds. Season to taste with salt and pepper.

Crustacean Oil Vinaigrette

Vinaigrette à l'huile de crustacés

I serve this vinaigrette at The Waterside Inn with a little dish of freshly cooked noodles and mixed shellfish — a veritable feast! It is also remarkably good served with poached lobster.

Serves 6
PREPARATION TIME: 5 MINUTES

Ingredients:
1/2 CUP CRUSTACEAN OIL (PAGE 47)
1 TABLESPOON WHOLEGRAIN MUSTARD
JUICE OF 1 LEMON
1 TABLESPOON SNIPPED TARRAGON LEAVES
SALT AND FRESHLY GROUND PEPPER

In a bowl, whisk all the ingredients together and season to taste with salt and pepper.

Truffle Vinaigrette

Vinaigrette à la truffe

This vinaigrette is divine with a salad of frisée or escarole, or with baby new potatoes, pasta, or tender young leeks, cooked briefly, refreshed, and served warm.

Serves 6
PREPARATION TIME: 5 MINUTES

Ingredients:
6 TABLESPOONS OLIVE OIL
2 TABLESPOONS RED WINE VINEGAR
2 OUNCES BLACK TRUFFLE, PREFERABLY RAW, MINCED
$1/2$ SMALL GARLIC CLOVE, MINCED
I ANCHOVY FILLET, RINSED IN COLD WATER AND MINCED
2 HARD-BOILED EGG YOLKS, RUBBED THROUGH A SIEVE OR MINCED
SALT AND FRESHLY GROUND PEPPER

Combine all the ingredients except the egg yolks in a bowl and mix with a spoon. Season with salt and pepper, and stir in the egg yolks just before serving.

Basil Vinaigrette

Vinaigrette au basilic

Use this vinaigrette with fresh pasta, green beans, and potato salad.

Serves 6
PREPARATION TIME: 5 MINUTES

Ingredients:
6 TABLESPOONS OLIVE OIL
2 TABLESPOONS RED WINE VINEGAR
$1/3$ CUP BASIL LEAVES, SNIPPED
I SMALL GARLIC CLOVE, MINCED
$1/4$ CUP MINCED SHALLOT
$1/4$ CUP DICED, PEELED, VERY RIPE TOMATO
SALT AND FRESHLY GROUND PEPPER

Put all the ingredients in a blender and whizz for 30 seconds. Season to taste with salt and pepper.

Tea Vinaigrette

Vinaigrette au thé

This light, refreshing dressing is perfect for a simple green salad. Choose the variety of tea according to your taste.

Serves 6
PREPARATION TIME: 5 MINUTES
COOKING TIME: ABOUT 2 MINUTES

Ingredients:
3 TABLESPOONS WHITE WINE VINEGAR
2 TEASPOONS CEYLON TEA LEAVES
$1/2$ CUP SUNFLOWER OIL
I TABLESPOON SNIPPED FLAT PARSLEY LEAVES
SALT AND FRESHLY GROUND PEPPER

In a small saucepan, bring the vinegar to a boil and immediately add the tea. Remove from the heat, cover the pan, and leave to cool for 10 minutes, then strain through a wire-mesh conical sieve into a bowl. Mix in the other ingredients with a spoon and season to taste.

Parmesan Vinaigrette

Vinaigrette à la crème et au parmesan

This dressing goes well with raw Belgian endive, spinach, or sliced mushrooms. If it seems too thick, thin it with a little vegetable stock or warm water.

Serves 6
PREPARATION TIME: 5 MINUTES

Ingredients:
I TEASPOON ENGLISH MUSTARD POWDER
2 TABLESPOONS CHAMPAGNE VINEGAR
6 TABLESPOONS HEAVY CREAM
$1/4$ CUP FRESHLY GRATED PARMESAN
I TABLESPOON SNIPPED CHIVES
SALT AND FRESHLY GROUND PEPPER

In a bowl, stir the mustard powder into the vinegar, then add the other ingredients and season.

Garlic Vinaigrette

Vinaigrette à l'ail

Cooked garlic is delicious and easy to digest. This vinaigrette with its delicate aroma is perfect for well-flavored mixed salads. Adjust the quantity of garlic to suit your own taste.

Serves 6
PREPARATION TIME: 5 MINUTES
COOKING TIME: ABOUT 10 MINUTES

Ingredients:
A HANDFUL OF COARSE COOKING SALT
6 FINE PLUMP GARLIC CLOVES
2 TABLESPOONS BALSAMIC VINEGAR
3 TABLESPOONS PEANUT OIL
3 TABLESPOONS WALNUT OIL
I TABLESPOON SNIPPED CHIVES
SALT AND FRESHLY GROUND PEPPER

Preheat the oven to 350°F. Spread the coarse salt in a small roasting pan, arrange the garlic cloves on top, and bake in the oven for 10 minutes. To check whether the garlic is cooked, insert the tip of a knife into the center; it should not meet any resistance. Remove the garlic cloves and use a fork to squash them out of their skins, one at a time. Place them on a plate.

Scrape the garlic purée into a bowl, add the vinegar and salt and pepper to taste, and whisk until amalgamated, then whisk in the two oils. Just before serving, stir in the chives.

Thai Vinaigrette with Lemon Grass

Vinaigrette thai à la citronnelle

This refreshing vinaigrette is ideal for seasoning crisp salad leaves like romaine or escarole. It makes an excellent dressing for rice noodles that have been rehydrated for 5 minutes in boiling water and refreshed in cold water. The addition of a few shrimp and some sesame seeds plus extra cilantro leaves makes it even more tempting.

Serves 10
PREPARATION TIME: 5 MINUTES, PLUS 2 HOURS' INFUSING

Ingredients:
I-INCH PIECE OF LEMON GRASS, MINCED
$1/3$ CUP CILANTRO LEAVES, FINELY SHREDDED
$1/4$ CUP FINELY SNIPPED CHIVES
2 TABLESPOONS THAI FISH SAUCE
I TEASPOON SOY SAUCE
I CUP SUNFLOWER OIL
$1/4$ CUP RICE WINE VINEGAR
FRESHLY GROUND BLACK PEPPER

Mix all the ingredients together in a bowl, season with pepper to taste, cover with plastic wrap, and leave the vinaigrette to infuse for 2 hours before using it.

SALAD OF RICE NOODLES AND SHRIMP, DRESSED WITH THAI VINAIGRETTE WITH LEMON GRASS, GARNISHED WITH CILANTRO

Cucumber Vinaigrette

Vinaigrette de concombre

This sauce is particularly nice in summer, served with green beans cooked al dente, *or thinly sliced button mushrooms.*

Serves 4
PREPARATION TIME: 10 MINUTES

Special equipment:
A MANDOLINE OR VEGETABLE GRATER

Ingredients:
1/2 POUND CUCUMBER
1/4 CUP MINCED SHALLOT
1 TEASPOON SNIPPED CHIVES
1 TEASPOON SNIPPED TARRAGON
1 TEASPOON SNIPPED FLAT-LEAF PARSLEY OR
CHERVIL
6 TABLESPOONS OLIVE OIL
2 TABLESPOONS RICE WINE VINEGAR
SALT AND FRESHLY GROUND PEPPER

Peel the cucumber with a potato peeler, halve it lengthwise, scoop out the seeds, and then slice it as thinly as possible on the mandoline or with the grater. Place in a bowl and add all the other ingredients, seasoning to taste with salt and pepper. Keep covered with plastic wrap until needed.

Saffron Vinaigrette

Vinaigrette au safran

This vinaigrette is especially delicious served with a mixed salad of tender leaves like corn salad or oakleaf lettuce garnished with scallops or warm grilled jumbo shrimp and a few cilantro leaves.

Serves 6
PREPARATION TIME: 5 MINUTES

Ingredients:
3 TABLESPOONS WHITE WINE VINEGAR
A LARGE PINCH OF SAFFRON THREADS
6 TABLESPOONS PEANUT OIL
1 TABLESPOON SESAME OIL
1 TEASPOON SOY SAUCE
SALT AND CAYENNE

In a small saucepan, warm the vinegar, add the saffron, remove from the heat, and infuse until cold. Whisk in all the other ingredients. The vinaigrette is now ready to serve.

Citrus Vinaigrette

Vinaigrette aux agrumes

This vinaigrette is good with all salads, particularly winter salad leaves such as escarole, frisée, *and radicchio.*

Serves 6
PREPARATION TIME: 5 MINUTES
COOKING TIME: 2 MINUTES

Ingredients:
ZEST OF 1 ORANGE, CUT IN FINE JULIENNE AND
BLANCHED
JUICE OF 1 ORANGE
1 TABLESPOON SUGAR
1 TEASPOON DIJON MUSTARD
ZEST OF 1 LEMON, CUT IN FINE JULIENNE AND
BLANCHED
JUICE OF 1 LEMON
6 TABLESPOONS PEANUT OIL
1 TABLESPOON MINCED PARSLEY
SALT AND FRESHLY GROUND PEPPER

Put the orange zest and juice and the sugar in a small saucepan and reduce by two-thirds over low heat. Keep at room temperature.

In a bowl, whisk together the mustard, lemon juice, and salt and pepper to taste. Whisk in the oil, then the reduced orange juice and zest. Just before serving, stir in the lemon zest and parsley.

Maman Roux's Vinaigrette

Vinaigrette Maman Roux

My mother's creamy vinaigrette has been a favorite of mine since childhood. It is excellent with garden lettuce and escarole.

Ingredients:
I TABLESPOON FRESHLY GRATED HORSERADISH
(BOTTLED WILL DO AT A PINCH)
JUICE OF I LEMON
I TABLESPOON WHITE WINE TARRAGON VINEGAR
6 TABLESPOONS HEAVY CREAM
1/3 CUP MINCED SHALLOT
I TABLESPOON SNIPPED TARRAGON LEAVES
SALT AND FRESHLY GROUND PEPPER

Whisk together the horseradish, lemon juice, vinegar, and seasoning. Gently stir in the cream. If necessary, thin the sauce with 1/2 tablespoon warm water. Add the shallot and tarragon just before mixing the dressing into the salad.

Warm Vinaigrette

Vinaigrette tiède

An excellent vinaigrette for substantial mixed salads. Base the dressing on the main ingredient — Américaine sauce for seafood, veal stock for rabbit, chicken livers, etc. Or use the deglazing juices from roast chicken or roast meats as a basis for the vinaigrette.

Serves 6
PREPARATION TIME: 5 MINUTES

Ingredients:
2 TABLESPOONS VEAL STOCK (PAGE I6)
OR AMÉRICAINE SAUCE (PAGE 90)
5 TABLESPOONS OLIVE OIL
3 TABLESPOONS SHERRY VINEGAR
I SPRIG OF THYME, MINCED
SALT AND FRESHLY GROUND PEPPER

Heat the veal stock or Américaine sauce to I40°-I75°F, then vigorously whisk in all the other ingredients. Serve the sauce immediately, while it is still tepid.

Anchovy Vinaigrette

Vinaigrette à l'anchois

Serve pan-fried fillets of red snapper or bass, or tender cooked artichokes, with a drizzle of this anchovy vinaigrette.

Serves 6
PREPARATION TIME: 5 MINUTES
COOKING TIME: ABOUT 5 MINUTES

Ingredients:
3 TABLESPOONS OLIVE OIL
I GARLIC CLOVE, MINCED
5 TABLESPOONS VEGETABLE STOCK (PAGE 22)
3 ANCHOVY FILLETS, MINCED
6 GREEN OLIVES, MINCED
2 TABLESPOONS BALSAMIC VINEGAR
SALT AND FRESHLY GROUND PEPPER

In a small saucepan, heat the oil to about 120°F, add the garlic, and infuse for 30 seconds. Add the stock and heat to 120°-140°F. Remove from the heat, whisk in the other ingredients, and season to taste. Serve tepid.

Low-Calorie Vinaigrette

Vinaigrette diététique

This flavorsome diet dressing marries well with most salads.

Serves 6
PREPARATION TIME: 5 MINUTES

Ingredients:
I TEASPOON WHOLEGRAIN MUSTARD
JUICE OF 2 LEMONS
1/2 CUP TOMATO JUICE, PREFERABLY FRESH
2 TABLESPOONS MINCED ONION
2 TABLESPOONS OLIVE OIL
I TABLESPOON SNIPPED BASIL OR TARRAGON LEAVES
SALT AND FRESHLY GROUND PEPPER

In a bowl, whisk together the mustard and lemon juice, then stir in all the other ingredients except the basil or tarragon; add this just before serving the vinaigrette.

Raspberry Vinegar

Vinaigre de framboise

The exceptionally fine aroma of this homemade vinegar makes the effort involved in preparing it well worthwhile. It can also be made with blackberries or black currants. Fruit vinegars make delicious dressings for modern composed salads, made with shellfish, raw vegetables, asparagus, artichokes, etc. Best of all, they can be used to deglaze the pan juices of pan-fried or roasted red meats and especially game; they add an intense and original depth of flavor to the sauce.

If the fruit is not very sweet, increase the quantity of sugar by 10-15%. The precise amount of vinegar obtained will depend on how much juice the fruit contains (this can vary by up to 30%).

Makes about 1 quart
PREPARATION TIME: 15 MINUTES, PLUS 48 HOURS' MACERATION
COOKING TIME: 1 HOUR

Ingredients:
3 1/2 POUNDS VERY RIPE RASPBERRIES, BLACKBERRIES, OR BLACK CURRANTS
5 CUPS WHITE WINE VINEGAR
2/3 CUP SUGAR
1 CUP WHITE DENATURED ALCOHOL OR COGNAC

Put half the fruit in a non-metallic bowl, cover with the vinegar (1), and cover the bowl with a dish towel or plastic wrap. Leave in a cool place for 24 hours. This is the first maceration.

After this time, place a fine-mesh sieve over a bowl and strain the juice from the first maceration of fruit (2), pressing very lightly with the back of a ladle to extract as much juice as possible without pushing through any pulp (3). You can use small quantities of the pulp in sauces for game, or simply throw it away. Add the remaining fruit to the extracted juice, then proceed as for the first maceration.

When the second 24 hours have elapsed, strain the juice from the fruit into a saucepan in the same way as before. Add the sugar and alcohol (4), and leave until the sugar has dissolved. Stand the pan on a sheet of parchment paper in a *bain-marie* filled with water, set over high heat, and bring to a boil. Lower the heat so that the water is just bubbling gently and cook the vinegar for 1 hour, adding more water to the *bain-marie* if necessary. The temperature of the vinegar should remain at a constant 195°F throughout; it must not boil (hence the need for a *bain-marie*). While it is cooking, skim the surface as often as necessary.

Transfer the vinegar to a non-metallic bowl and leave in a cool place until cold. Strain it through cheesecloth and a funnel into a bottle and cork it. The vinegar is now ready to use, and will keep for 3 weeks in the refrigerator.

STRAIN THE VINEGAR THROUGH CHEESECLOTH AND A FUNNEL INTO A BOTTLE

Crustacean Oil

Huile de crustacés

This wonderfully delicate oil is one of my favorites. It makes a superb dressing for fantasy seafood salads or warm asparagus spears.

Makes about 1 quart
PREPARATION TIME: 20 MINUTES, PLUS 3 HOURS'
DRYING
STERILIZATION TIME: 35–45 MINUTES

Special equipment:
A 1-QUART CANNING JAR. IDEALLY, THIS SHOULD BE
NEW – IF NOT, IT MUST BE SCRUPULOUSLY CLEAN

Ingredients:
2¹/4 POUNDS *LANGOUSTINES* (DUBLIN BAY PRAWNS) OR
CRAYFISH, COOKED IN SALTED WATER
¹/2 HEAD OF GARLIC, UNPEELED
1 SPRIG OF THYME
2 BAY LEAVES
1 SMALL BUNCH OF TARRAGON
1 TEASPOON WHOLE WHITE PEPPERCORNS
¹/2 TEASPOON WHOLE CORIANDER SEEDS
APPROXIMATELY 1 QUART PEANUT OR OLIVE OIL
SALT

Preheat the oven to 250°F. Remove the eyes of the crustaceans, and separate the heads, claws, and tails. Keep the tails to use as a garnish for fish or serve in a salad as an hors d'oeuvre. Roughly chop the heads and claws with a chef's knife, put them in a roasting pan, and place in the oven to dry for 3 hours. Put the dried heads and claws into the canning jar with the aromatics, fill up with oil to within 1 inch of the top, and seal the lid carefully.

CRUSTACEAN OIL IS
DELICIOUS SERVED WITH
WARM ASPARAGUS

To sterilize the oil, you will need a pot at least as tall as the jar. Line the bottom and sides of the pan with foil; this will protect the glass, which might explode if it should knock against the side of the pan. Put in the jar and pour in enough water, salted with 1 cup salt per quart of water, to come up to the level of the oil in the jar, but not to submerge it. Bring the water to a boil over high heat and boil for 35–45 minutes, depending on the size of the jar.

After sterilization, leave the jar at room temperature until completely cold, then refrigerate for at least 8 days before using the oil. It will keep for months in the sealed sterile jar if stored in a cool place. Once opened, decant the oil into a bottle; it will keep for several weeks in the refrigerator.

ABOVE: SEPARATE THE TAILS
FROM THE HEADS AND CLAWS
OF THE CRUSTACEANS

LEFT: PUT THE HEADS AND
CLAWS, ROUGHLY CHOPPED,
IN A ROASTING PAN

PUT THE DRIED HEADS AND CLAWS
INTO A CLEAN CANNING JAR WITH
THE AROMATICS

FILL THE JAR WITH OIL TO WITHIN
1 INCH OF THE TOP

STERILIZE THE JAR OF OIL IN
A FOIL-LINED PAN OF
BOILING SALTED WATER FOR
35–45 MINUTES

Hot-Pepper Oil

Huile au parfum de piment

Use this oil to add spiciness and zing to pizzas or vinaigrettes.

Makes 2 cups
PREPARATION TIME: 5 MINUTES
COOKING TIME: ABOUT 5 MINUTES

Ingredients:
2 CUPS OLIVE OIL
1/3 CUP MINCED FRESH RED CHILI PEPPER
1 SPRIG OF THYME
1 BAY LEAF
1 UNPEELED GARLIC CLOVE

In a saucepan, heat the oil to about 175°F. Add all the other ingredients and cover the pan. Immediately remove from the heat and leave the oil to cool. Once cold, pass it through a wire-mesh conical sieve, then pour into a bottle and cork it.

Chive-Flavored Oil

Huile au parfum de ciboulette

Drizzle this oil over grilled fish or add some to a vinaigrette to give a pronounced chive flavor.

Makes 2 cups
PREPARATION TIME: 5 MINUTES
COOKING TIME: ABOUT 5 MINUTES

Ingredients:
2 CUPS OLIVE OIL
1 CUP SNIPPED CHIVES

In a saucepan, heat the oil to about 175°F, add the chives, and cover the pan. Immediately, remove from the heat and leave the oil to cool. Once cold, whizz in a blender for 30 seconds, then pass the oil through a wire-mesh conical sieve, pour into a bottle, and top it with a cork. It will keep for several days.

Bois Boudran Sauce

Sauce Bois Boudran

An excellent sauce for roast chicken or poussin, Bois Boudran sauce can also be used to coat a salmon or lightly poached trout just before serving. I have loved this sauce ever since the days when I cooked for the Rothschild family.

Serves 6
PREPARATION TIME: 5 MINUTES

Ingredients:
2/3 CUP PEANUT OIL
3 1/2 TABLESPOONS WINE VINEGAR
5 TABLESPOONS TOMATO KETCHUP
1 TEASPOON WORCESTERSHIRE SAUCE
5 DROPS OF HOT-PEPPER SAUCE
2/3 CUP CHOPPED SHALLOTS
2 TABLESPOONS FINELY SNIPPED CHERVIL
2 TABLESPOONS FINELY SNIPPED CHIVES
1/2 CUP FINELY SNIPPED TARRAGON
SALT AND FRESHLY GROUND PEPPER

Combine the oil, vinegar, a pinch of salt, and three turns of the pepper mill in a bowl. Stir with a small whisk, then add the ketchup, Worcestershire sauce, pepper sauce, chopped shallots, and all the snipped herbs. Adjust the seasoning with salt and pepper and keep at room temperature; the sauce is ready to use right away, but it can also be kept in an airtight container in the refrigerator for 3 days.

POACHED SALMON
WITH BOIS BOUDRAN
SAUCE

Pistou Sauce

Sauce au pistou

Pistou smells as good as it tastes. Use it to perfume Mediterranean soups and steamed fish. Its powerful, intoxicating flavor also goes well with pasta.

Serves 6
PREPARATION TIME: 10 MINUTES

Ingredients:
4 GARLIC CLOVES, PEELED, HALVED,
AND GREEN SHOOT REMOVED
20 BASIL LEAVES
1 CUP FRESHLY GRATED PARMESAN
2/3 CUP OLIVE OIL
SALT AND FRESHLY GROUND PEPPER

In a small mortar, crush the garlic to a purée (1) with a pinch of salt (or use a blender). Add the basil and crush or blend to a homogeneous paste (2). Add the Parmesan (3), then trickle in the olive oil in a steady stream, stirring continuously with the pestle, as though you were making mayonnaise (4). Work the sauce until smooth (5). Season to taste with salt and pepper.

Use the pistou immediately, or transfer it to a bowl and cover with plastic wrap. It will keep in the refrigerator for several days.

PESTO: If you add 1/4 cup toasted pine nuts with the basil, you will obtain Italian pesto, which has a firmer, richer consistency. Pesto is perfect stirred into a risotto just before serving, and has many other uses.

PISTOU IS DELICIOUS STIRRED INTO VEGETABLE SOUPS

Piquant Fromage Blanc Sauce

Sauce piquant au fromage blanc

This sauce is most agreeable served with a cold vegetable terrine or a warm pizza-style tomato and zucchini tart.

Serves 8
PREPARATION TIME: 5 MINUTES

Ingredients:
14 OUNCES (ABOUT 1 3/4 CUPS) FROMAGE BLANC,
WHICHEVER FAT CONTENT YOU PREFER
SEEDS FROM 2 PASSION FRUIT, SCOOPED OUT WITH A
SPOON
1/4 CUP RASPBERRY VINEGAR,
HOMEMADE (PAGE 44) OR STORE-BOUGHT
1 TABLESPOON FINELY SNIPPED LEMON VERBENA
1/2 TABLESPOON SOFT GREEN PEPPERCORNS, WELL
DRAINED AND CHOPPED
SALT AND CAYENNE

Put all the ingredients in a bowl and mix together with a spoon. Season with salt and plenty of cayenne.

Avocado Sauce

Sauce à l'avocat

Serve this sauce as a dip for raw vegetables, such as carrots, cauliflower, cucumber, or radishes, or with cold cooked shrimp or mussels.

Serves 6
PREPARATION TIME: 5 MINUTES

Ingredients:
1 AVOCADO, ABOUT 10 OUNCES, PEELED AND PITTED
1 1/4 CUPS PLAIN YOGURT
3 TABLESPOONS SNIPPED DILL
2 TABLESPOONS LEMON JUICE
1 TEASPOON STRONG DIJON MUSTARD
A SMALL PINCH OF CURRY POWDER
SALT AND FRESHLY GROUND PEPPER

Combine all the ingredients in a blender and whizz for 30 seconds. Adjust the seasoning with salt and pepper.

Ravigote Sauce

Sauce ravigote

This sauce gives an extra lift to variety meats such as brains, tongue, feet, head, etc. I also like to serve it with potatoes boiled in their skins — leave your guests to peel their own potatoes and dip them in the sauce as they eat.

Serves 6
PREPARATION TIME: 5 MINUTES

Ingredients:
6 TABLESPOONS PEANUT OR SUNFLOWER OIL
2 TABLESPOONS WHITE WINE VINEGAR
1 TABLESPOON SMALL CAPERS (CHOP THEM IF THEY
ARE LARGE)
1 TABLESPOON FINELY DICED CORNICHONS OR SMALL
GHERKINS
1/4 CUP FINELY SNIPPED FINES HERBES (PAGE 10)
2 TABLESPOONS MINCED ONION
SALT AND FRESHLY GROUND PEPPER

Combine all the ingredients in a bowl and mix thoroughly.

Oregano and Sun-Dried Tomato Sauce with Basil Oil

Sauce à l'origan et aux tomates séchées, à l'huile de basilic

This sun-dried tomato sauce makes an excellent accompaniment to grilled veal chops and tournedos, or robust fish like tuna or monkfish.

Serves 8
PREPARATION TIME: 10 MINUTES

Ingredients:
3/4 CUP SUN-DRIED TOMATOES IN OLIVE OIL
6 OUNCES VERY RIPE FRESH TOMATOES
I CUP CHICKEN STOCK (PAGE 18)
3 TABLESPOONS BALSAMIC VINEGAR
I TABLESPOON MINCED OREGANO LEAVES
SALT AND FRESHLY GROUND PEPPER

For the basil oil:
1/4 CUP EXTRA VIRGIN OLIVE OIL
1/4 CUP FRESH BASIL LEAVES

Combine the sun-dried and fresh tomatoes, chicken stock, and balsamic vinegar in the bowl of a food processor. Whizz for 2 minutes, then strain the sauce through a conical sieve into a bowl. Add the chopped oregano, and season with salt and pepper.

To make the basil oil, put the oil and basil in the clean bowl of the food processor. Season to taste with salt and pepper, and whizz for 2 minutes. Pour the oil straight into a bowl (do not strain it).

Serve the tomato sauce either tepid or cold, poured in a ribbon around the meat or fish, then sprinkled with a few drops of basil oil.

Sauce Vierge

I serve this sauce with lobster cappelletti, steamed fillets of red mullet and sea bass, and fresh pasta.

Serves 6
PREPARATION TIME: 5 MINUTES

Ingredients:
I CUP OLIVE OIL
1/2 CUP FINELY DICED TOMATOES, PEELED AND SEEDED
JUICE OF I LEMON
2 TABLESPOONS SNIPPED BASIL LEAVES
I TABLESPOON SNIPPED CHERVIL LEAVES
I GARLIC CLOVE, MINCED
6 CORIANDER SEEDS, CRUSHED
SALT AND FRESHLY GROUND PEPPER

Combine the ingredients in a bowl, mix gently, and season. Just before serving, warm the sauce to about 85°–105°F.

CHAPTER 4

Flavored butters are tasty, simple to prepare, and come in a range of attractive colors, from pastel to vibrant, depending on their composition. They can be used instead of a sauce (allow 2 tablespoons per person) and as a topping for vegetables or poached, pan-fried, or grilled fish and meat.

*F*lavored Butters

& Vegetable Coulis

I usually roll the butters into a sausage shape, using plastic wrap, but if you prefer, they can be piped into rosettes using a pastry bag with a fluted tip. Many make delicious canapés: soften the butter slightly and spread or pipe it onto small toasted croûtons.

The butters are at their most flavorsome made just before serving and firmed up for a few minutes in the refrigerator, but they can be kept refrigerated for three or four days, or frozen for several weeks. That way, you can always add extra flavor to a dish in a matter of moments.

I use my flavored butters to enhance a sauce, to refine it (with foie-gras butter, for example), or to personalize it as the mood takes me with the flavor of vegetables, herbs, or shellfish. This chapter contains my particular favorites, but you can create dozens of other butters, using mustard, olives, truffles, tomato ... let your imagination run riot.

Vegetable coulis are also extremely useful and taste wonderful. These are champion sauces — light, insubstantial, and quick to prepare. Some contain cream, but this can be replaced by fromage blanc if you prefer. Do not cook this in the sauce, but add it at the last moment and give it just a brief bubble. These coulis should be served in a sauceboat, or spread thinly over a plate and topped with the accompanying fish or meat.

Vegetable Butter

Beurre de légumes

This butter is ideal as a liaison for a béchamel sauce (page 128) or chicken velouté (page 132), lifting them out of the ordinary with its special flavor and perfect color. A few pats make a most delicious topping for boiled potatoes.

Makes about 1 cup
PREPARATION TIME: 10 MINUTES

Ingredients:
5 OUNCES VEGETABLES OF YOUR CHOICE, E.G.
CARROTS, GREEN BEANS, OR ASPARAGUS
10 TABLESPOONS BUTTER, SOFTENED

Peel or trim and wash the vegetables, and cook them in lightly salted water until tender. Refresh, drain, and pat dry with a cloth.

Put the cooked vegetables and the butter in a food processor and whizz for about 3 minutes, scraping the ingredients into the center of the bowl every minute to make a homogeneous mixture. If you don't have a food processor, use a pestle and mortar.

Using a plastic scraper, rub the flavored butter through a drum sieve to eliminate any vegetable fibers. Using plastic wrap, roll it into one or two sausage shapes, and refrigerate or freeze until ready to use.

Maître d'Hôtel Butter

Beurre maître d'hôtel

This classic topping remains a favorite for grilled meat or fish.

Makes about 3/4 cup
PREPARATION TIME: 5 MINUTES

Ingredients:
1/2 CUP PARSLEY, CHOPPED
10 TABLESPOONS BUTTER, SOFTENED
JUICE OF 1/2 LEMON
SALT
A PINCH OF CAYENNE OR FRESHLY GROUND BLACK PEPPER

Using a wooden spoon, work the parsley into the butter, then mix in the lemon juice. Season to taste and, using plastic wrap, roll the butter into one or two sausage shapes. Refrigerate or freeze until needed.

Horseradish Butter

Beurre de raifort

Finish a sauce Albert (page 132) with this delicious butter, or use it to pep up a béchamel (page 128). It also goes well with any grilled white meat.

Makes just under 1 cup
PREPARATION TIME: 7 MINUTES

Ingredients:
1/4 CUP FRESHLY GRATED HORSERADISH
10 TABLESPOONS BUTTER, SOFTENED
SALT AND FRESHLY GROUND PEPPER

Pulverize the horseradish with a pestle in a mortar, adding the butter a little at a time. When it is all well mixed, use a plastic scraper to rub the seasoned butter through a drum sieve and season to taste with salt and pepper. Using plastic wrap, roll it into one or two sausage shapes, and refrigerate or freeze until needed.

Langoustine Butter

Beurre de langoustines

Enrich fish sauces with this butter. It makes wonderful canapés spread on toast croûtons and topped with prawns or shrimp.

Makes about 2 cups
PREPARATION TIME: 15 MINUTES
COOKING TIME: ABOUT 20 MINUTES

Ingredients:
4 TABLESPOONS BUTTER, PREFERABLY CLARIFIED
(PAGE 31)
1 SMALL CARROT, FINELY DICED
1 MEDIUM ONION, FINELY DICED
12 *LANGOUSTINES* (DUBLIN BAY PRAWNS) OR
CRAYFISH, LIVE IF POSSIBLE
5 TABLESPOONS COGNAC OR ARMAGNAC
1 CUP WHITE WINE
1 SMALL BOUQUET GARNI (PAGE 10)
2 PINCHES OF CAYENNE
SOFTENED BUTTER, 75% OF THE WEIGHT OF THE
COOKED CRUSTACEAN HEADS AND CLAWS
SALT AND FRESHLY GROUND PEPPER

Melt the clarified butter in a deep frying pan, add the diced carrot and onion, and sweat until soft. Using a slotted spoon, transfer the vegetables to a bowl, leaving the cooking butter in the pan.

Put the crustaceans in the pan and sauté over high heat for 2 minutes. Add the cognac, ignite it, and then moisten with the white wine. Add the cooked diced vegetables, bouquet garni, a little cayenne, and a small pinch of salt. Cook gently over low heat for 10 minutes. Tip all the contents of the pan into a bowl and leave to cool completely at room temperature.

To make the flavored butter, separate the prawn or crayfish heads and tails. Keep the tails for another use (as an hors d'oeuvre salad or canapés, for example). Gather up the heads and claws, and the creamy flesh ("butter") from the heads, and weigh them. Put them in a food processor or blender with 75% of their weight of softened butter and the diced vegetables, and whizz until mushy. Using a plastic scraper, rub through a drum sieve and season to taste. Using plastic wrap, roll the flavored butter into one or two sausage shapes, and refrigerate or freeze until needed.

Pistachio Butter

Beurre de pistaches

I use this butter in my Sauternes sauce with pistachios (page 102) or add it to a hollandaise (page 116) to give a touch of mellowness.

Makes about 1 cup
PREPARATION TIME: 7 MINUTES

Ingredients:
3/4 CUP SKINNED PISTACHIO NUTS
10 TABLESPOONS BUTTER, SOFTENED
SALT AND FRESHLY GROUND PEPPER

Pound the pistachios to a paste with 1 tablespoon water in a mortar or food processor. Add all the butter at once, mix, and season, then rub through a drum sieve with a plastic scraper. Using plastic wrap, roll the pistachio butter into one or two sausage shapes, and refrigerate or freeze until ready to use.

Anchovy Butter

Beurre d'anchois

Use this delicious butter on grilled fish, or spread it on toast canapés and top with a julienne of anchovy fillets.

Makes about 3/4 cup
PREPARATION TIME: 7 MINUTES

Ingredients:
2 OUNCES ANCHOVY FILLETS IN OIL
10 TABLESPOONS BUTTER, SOFTENED
SALT AND FRESHLY GROUND PEPPER

Chop the anchovy fillets or pound them in a mortar. Using a wooden spoon, mix them into the butter and, using a plastic scraper, rub through a drum sieve or whizz in a food processor. Season, being circumspect with the salt because the anchovies already contain plenty. Use plastic wrap to roll the butter into one or two sausage shapes, and refrigerate or freeze until ready to use.

POUND TO A PASTE

RUB THE PASTE THROUGH
A DRUM SIEVE

THE BUTTER SHOULD
NOT CONTAIN ANY HARD
GRAINS OF CHEESE

Goat-Cheese Butter

Beurre de fromage de chèvre

Pats of goat-cheese butter make an appetizing topping for grilled white meats, like veal cutlets or chicken breasts. The butter is also delicious with pasta: mix it in just before serving and add a little snipped basil or flat-leaf parsley to enhance the flavor of the cheesy butter.

Makes about 1 ⅓ cups
PREPARATION TIME: 5 MINUTES

Ingredients:
5 OUNCES FRESH OR SEMI-HARD GOAT CHEESE,
WHICHEVER YOU PREFER
10 TABLESPOONS BUTTER, SOFTENED

Cut up the goat cheese, put it in a mortar or food processor with the butter, and pound with a pestle or process for about 3 minutes, scraping the butter and cheese toward the center of the bowl every minute to obtain a completely homogeneous mixture. Using a plastic scraper, rub the flavored butter through a drum sieve to eliminate any hard grains of cheese, then, using plastic wrap, roll it into one or two sausage shapes. Refrigerate or freeze until ready to use.

RIGHT: COMBINE THE CHEESE
AND BUTTER IN A MORTAR

PUT THE BUTTER ONTO A
SHEET OF PLASTIC WRAP

ROLL THE BUTTER INTO A
SAUSAGE SHAPE IN THE
PLASTIC WRAP

Shrimp Butter

Beurre de crevettes

LEFT: WASH THE SHRIMP IN
COLD WATER

Pats of shrimp butter add a special something to pan-fried or grilled fish. It can also be used to enrich a fish sauce, or spread on toasted croûtons to make canapés. For extra zing, add a pinch of cayenne.

Makes about 1 cup
PREPARATION TIME: 10 MINUTES

Ingredients:
5 OUNCES VERY FRESH COOKED SHRIMP
10 TABLESPOONS BUTTER, SOFTENED
CAYENNE (OPTIONAL)

PROCESS WITH BUTTER
TO A PASTE

Rinse the shrimp in cold water, leaving any eggs attached, drain, and pat dry in a dish towel.

Place the shrimp in a blender with the butter and a pinch of cayenne, if you like. Process for about 3 minutes, scraping the ingredients into the center of the bowl every minute, to obtain a homogeneous mixture. If you prefer, you can use a pestle and mortar instead of a blender.

Using a plastic scraper, rub the flavored butter through a drum sieve to eliminate the shrimp shells. Using plastic wrap, roll it into one or two sausage shapes, and refrigerate or freeze until ready to use.

PUT THE SHRIMP IN A
BLENDER

RUB THE SHRIMP BUTTER
THROUGH A SIEVE

PAN-FRIED FISH TOPPED WITH SHRIMP
BUTTER

Roquefort Butter

Beurre de roquefort

Use this butter as a delicious spread for toast canapés, or whisk it into a fish velouté to add extra character and piquancy. This is particularly good with cooked shelled mussels served in ramekins. A tablespoon of Roquefort butter can also be added to a sauce for poultry.

Makes about 1 cup
PREPARATION TIME: 5 MINUTES

Ingredients:
4 OUNCES ROQUEFORT
10 TABLESPOONS BUTTER, SOFTENED
FRESHLY GROUND PEPPER

Crumble the Roquefort and work it into the softened butter with a wooden spoon. Using a plastic scraper, rub it through a drum sieve and season with pepper to taste. Using plastic wrap, roll the butter into one or two sausage shapes, and refrigerate or freeze until ready to use.

Barbecue Butter

Beurre barbecue

This butter enhances the flavor of any barbecued meats. Brush it over the cooked meat just before serving.

Makes about 3/4 cup
PREPARATION TIME: 7 MINUTES

Ingredients:
10 TABLESPOONS BUTTER, SOFTENED
1 TABLESPOON CHILI SAUCE
1 TABLESPOON HONEY
1 TABLESPOON LEMON JUICE
1/4 CUP MINT LEAVES, SHREDDED
SALT AND FRESHLY GROUND PEPPER

Using a wooden spoon, mix the ingredients one a time into the softened butter, adding the mint last of all. Season to taste. The butter is ready to use immediately. Keep it at room temperature.

Caviar Butter

Beurre de caviar

Serve this flavorsome, delicate butter in a sauceboat to accompany grilled fillets of sole. It is best to use it on the day it is made, without refrigerating or freezing it.

Makes about 1 cup
PREPARATION TIME: 5 MINUTES

Ingredients:
2 OUNCES CAVIAR, PREFERABLY PRESSED (OTHERWISE
USE SEVRUGA)
10 TABLESPOONS BUTTER, SOFTENED
SALT AND FRESHLY GROUND PEPPER

Using a wooden spoon, mix the caviar into the butter, then, using a plastic scraper, rub it through a drum sieve. Season to taste and use on the same day.

Crab Butter

Beurre de tourteau

Serve crab butter on toast canapés, or use it to add extra body to sauces for scallops and seafood.

Makes about 1 1/3 cups
PREPARATION TIME: 7 MINUTES

Ingredients:
1 HEAPED CUP LUMP CRAB MEAT
10 TABLESPOONS BUTTER, SOFTENED
1 TABLESPOON COGNAC
1 TEASPOON HARISSA, OR 5 DROPS OF
HOT-PEPPER SAUCE
JUICE OF 1/2 LEMON
SALT AND FRESHLY GROUND PEPPER

Whizz the crab meat and butter in a blender for 3 minutes. Rub through a drum sieve. Then, with a wooden spoon, mix in the cognac, harissa or pepper sauce, and the lemon juice, and season to taste. Using plastic wrap, roll the butter into one or two sausage shapes, and refrigerate or freeze until needed.

Paprika Butter

Beurre de paprika

This butter is perfect served with veal, turkey, or chicken cutlets.

Makes about ³/₄ cup
PREPARATION TIME: 10 MINUTES

Ingredients:
1¹/₂ TABLESPOONS BUTTER
2 TABLESPOONS MINCED ONION
10 TABLESPOONS BUTTER, SOFTENED
¹/₂-1 TABLESPOON PAPRIKA, ACCORDING TO TASTE
SALT AND FRESHLY GROUND PEPPER

Melt the 1¹/₂ tablespoons butter in a small saucepan, add the onion, and sweat gently for 2 minutes. Leave to cool. As soon as the onion is completely cold, mix it into the softened butter with a wooden spoon. Add the paprika and season to taste with salt and pepper. Using a plastic scraper, rub the flavored butter through a sieve or whizz in a food processor. Using plastic wrap, roll it into one or two sausage shapes, and refrigerate or freeze until needed.

CURRY BUTTER: This can be made in the same way; just double the quantity of onion and the butter to sweat it in, and replace the paprika with 1-2 tablespoons curry powder, according to your taste. Add the curry to the onions after 1 minute, not directly to the softened butter. Curry butter can be used with the same meats as paprika butter, and also with grilled pork chops.

Foie-Gras Butter

Beurre de foie gras

This creamy, delicate, and tasty butter is excellent on toast canapés. A few pats add a wonderful flavor to a grilled steak, but — best of all — it gives a superb velvety, unctuous finish to many sauces, such as allemande (page 139), Périgueux (page 144), and port-wine (page 74).

Makes about 1 cup
PREPARATION TIME: 5 MINUTES

Ingredients:
7 TABLESPOONS BUTTER, SOFTENED
3¹/₂ OUNCES TERRINE OR BALLOTINE OF DUCK OR
GOOSE FOIE GRAS
2 TABLESPOONS ARMAGNAC OR COGNAC
SALT AND FRESHLY GROUND PEPPER

Mix all the ingredients with a wooden spoon, seasoning to taste with salt and pepper. Using a plastic scraper, rub through a drum sieve or whizz in a blender. Using plastic wrap, roll the butter into one or two sausage shapes, and refrigerate or freeze until needed.

Red-Pepper Butter

Beurre de poivron rouge

Like anchovy butter, red-pepper butter is excellent spread on toast canapés, and accompanies poached fish extremely well. Whisked into sauces, such as hollandaise (page 116), béchamel (page 128), or devil sauce (page 152), this butter will enhance the flavor and color and add a touch of originality.

Makes about 1 cup
PREPARATION TIME: 10 MINUTES

Ingredients:
1 1/2 TABLESPOONS BUTTER
1/2 CUP FINELY DICED RED BELL PEPPER
1 SPRIG OF THYME
10 TABLESPOONS BUTTER, SOFTENED
SALT AND FRESHLY GROUND BLACK PEPPER

Melt the 1 1/2 tablespoons butter in a small saucepan and add the diced bell pepper and thyme. Sweat gently for 5 minutes, then leave at room temperature until cold. Mix the cooked bell pepper into the butter with a wooden spoon, then use a plastic scraper to rub the butter through a drum sieve, or whizz it in a blender. Using plastic wrap, roll the butter into one or two sausage shapes, and refrigerate or freeze until ready to use.

Asparagus Coulis

Coulis d'asperges

This delicious sauce is almost as light as a nage. I add some asparagus tips at the last moment and serve it with delicate steamed fish, or pour it around my vegetable lasagne to make a dish that even non-vegetarians love.

Serves 8
PREPARATION TIME: 10 MINUTES
COOKING TIME: ABOUT 40 MINUTES

Ingredients:
3/4 POUND ASPARAGUS SPEARS, PREFERABLY SMALL ONES
4 TABLESPOONS BUTTER
2/3 CUP CHOPPED SHALLOTS
1 SPRIG OF THYME
1 1/4 CUPS CHICKEN STOCK (PAGE 18) OR WATER
2 CUPS HEAVY CREAM
1 TEASPOON SOY SAUCE (OPTIONAL)
SALT AND FRESHLY GROUND PEPPER

Peel the asparagus stalks with a vegetable peeler. Cut off the tips and blanch them in boiling salted water. Refresh, drain, and set aside. Chop the stalks and leave them raw.

In a thick-bottomed saucepan, melt the butter, add the chopped asparagus stalks and shallot, and sweat gently for 5 minutes. Add the thyme and chicken stock or water and cook over medium heat for 15 minutes. Pour in the cream, increase the heat to high, and reduce the coulis by one-third. Whizz in a blender for 3 minutes, then pass through a conical sieve. Season with salt and pepper to taste, adding the soy sauce if you wish. Add the blanched asparagus tips. Keep the coulis warm until needed.

Chilled Vegetable Coulis

Coulis de légumes glacés

These chilled vegetable coulis make excellent accompaniments to cold poached fish served as part of a buffet, or by themselves as a summer hors d'oeuvre. I sometimes serve three different coulis (carrot, celeriac, and pea) as an attractive, mellow amuse-gueule, placing a tablespoon of each on a small plate, to be eaten with a teaspoon.

Serves 6
PREPARATION TIME: 10 MINUTES
COOKING TIME: 5–20 MINUTES, DEPENDING ON THE VEGETABLES

Ingredients:
3/4 POUND CARROTS OR CELERIAC (CELERY ROOT),
PEELED AND DICED, OR
3/4 POUND GREEN BEANS, OR 3 1/3 CUPS SHELLED
FRESH PEAS
2 CUPS HEAVY CREAM
SALT AND FRESHLY GROUND PEPPER

Cook your chosen vegetable in boiling salted water until tender. Drain and whizz in a blender with 1/2 cup cream to make a very smooth purée. Transfer to a bowl and leave to cool, stirring from time to time. Using a whisk, gently stir in the rest of the cream. Season the coulis to taste with salt and pepper, and chill in the refrigerator until needed.

Raw Tomato Coulis

Coulis de tomates crues

I adore this coulis served with cold poached eggs or as a sauce for cold pasta — a simple, refreshing summer dish that is very quick to prepare.

Serves 6
PREPARATION TIME: 5 MINUTES

Ingredients:
3/4 POUND VERY RIPE TOMATOES, PURÉED
THEN RUBBED THROUGH A SIEVE TO GIVE
ABOUT 1 CUP JUICE AND PULP
1/4 CUP SHERRY VINEGAR (PREFERABLY)
OR BALSAMIC VINEGAR
8 CORIANDER SEEDS, CRUSHED
12 BASIL LEAVES, SHREDDED
1 TEASPOON TOMATO PASTE (OPTIONAL)
7 TABLESPOONS OLIVE OIL
SALT AND FRESHLY GROUND PEPPER

Put all the ingredients in a bowl, except the basil leaves. Mix with a whisk, and season with salt and pepper, then add the basil. The coulis is ready to serve. Alternatively, transfer it to an airtight container and refrigerate; it will keep well for 3 days.

Cooked Tomato Coulis

Coulis de tomates cuites

This tomato coulis is extremely versatile, and I use it frequently in my kitchen. It is divine spread over a plate and topped with grilled fish. Alternatively add a small quantity to a fish sauce or, better still, a béchamel (page 128) for a gratin of fresh pasta.

Serves 4
PREPARATION TIME: 5 MINUTES
COOKING TIME: ABOUT 1 HOUR

Ingredients:
$^2/_3$ CUP OLIVE OIL
2 GARLIC CLOVES, CRUSHED
$^1/_2$ CUP MINCED SHALLOTS
1 SMALL BOUQUET GARNI (PAGE 10),
CONTAINING PLENTY OF THYME
$1^1/_2$ POUNDS VERY RIPE TOMATOES,
PEELED, SEEDED, AND CHOPPED
1 TABLESPOON TOMATO PASTE (ONLY IF THE
TOMATOES ARE NOT RIPE ENOUGH)
A PINCH OF SUGAR
6 PEPPERCORNS, CRUSHED
SALT

In a thick-bottomed saucepan, warm the olive oil with the garlic, shallot, and bouquet garni. After 2 minutes, add the tomatoes, tomato paste if needed, sugar, and crushed peppercorns. Cook very gently for about 1 hour, stirring occasionally with a wooden spoon, until all the moisture has evaporated. Remove the bouquet garni and whizz the contents of the pan in a blender to make a smooth purée. Season to taste. The coulis is ready to use immediately, but you can keep it in an airtight container in the refrigerator for 5 days.

If the sauce is to be served plain, after reheating, add a little olive oil just before serving.

HOW TO PEEL TOMATOES: Cut a cross in the top of the tomatoes and gouge out the cores. Drop the tomatoes into boiling water and leave until the skin starts to split (10–20 seconds), then take them out (1) and plunge them into ice water (2). Lift out the tomatoes with a draining spoon (3) and slip off the skins (4).

ADD THE CHOPPED TOMATOES TO THE SOFTENED SHALLOTS

COOK THE TOMATOES UNTIL ALL THE MOISTURE HAS EVAPORATED

PUT THE CONTENTS OF THE PAN, EXCEPT THE BOUQUET GARNI, INTO A BLENDER AND WHIZZ INTO A SMOOTH PASTE

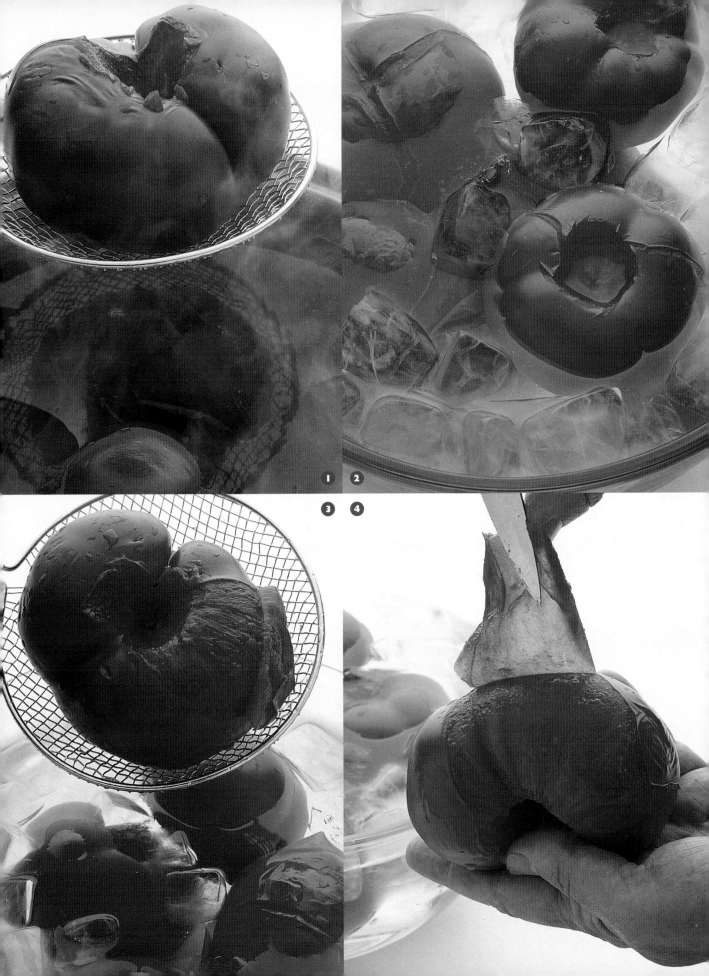

1 2

3 4

Light Carrot Coulis

Coulis léger de carottes

This coulis is almost like a jus and should be eaten with a spoon. It goes well with pan-fried scallops and grilled poultry breasts, and also with rice pilaff. I serve it with carrot tart, which always appeals to my vegetarian customers. For them, I omit the veal stock and thicken the sauce with a little beurre manié (page 31).

Serves 6
PREPARATION TIME: 5 MINUTES
COOKING TIME: ABOUT 10 MINUTES

Ingredients:
3 CARROTS, TOTAL WEIGHT ABOUT $^1/_2$ POUND
JUICE OF 2 ORANGES
1 CUP VEAL STOCK (PAGE 16)
1 TEASPOON FRESHLY GRATED GINGER
4 TABLESPOONS BUTTER, CHILLED AND DICED
SALT AND FRESHLY GROUND PEPPER

Peel the carrots and cut them into small pieces, then whizz them in a food processor with the orange juice and veal stock for 3 minutes. Transfer to a saucepan, set over high heat, and reduce the coulis for about 10 minutes, until it lightly coats the back of a spoon. Add the ginger, take the pan off the heat, and whisk in the butter, a little at a time. Season the coulis to taste, pass it through a conical sieve, and serve immediately.

Endive and champagne Coulis

Coulis d'endives au champagne

I love this light, delicate sauce served with poached poussin, chicken, or capon, or poured over cauliflower florets in shallow ramekins. The cauliflower must be very tender and not at all crunchy. In season, I put a little truffle in the sauce, which adds a stunning extra dimension — definitely worth trying!

Serves 4
PREPARATION TIME: 20 MINUTES
COOKING TIME: ABOUT 30 MINUTES

Ingredients:
2 HEADS OF BELGIAN ENDIVE, TOTAL WEIGHT ABOUT
7 OUNCES
4 TABLESPOONS BUTTER
$^3/_4$ CUP THINLY SLICED BUTTON MUSHROOMS
JUICE OF $^1/_2$ LEMON
A PINCH OF SUGAR
$1^1/_4$ CUPS CHAMPAGNE
1 CUP HEAVY CREAM
1 TABLESPOON TRUFFLE JUICE, OR 1 OUNCE
TRUFFLES, MINCED (OPTIONAL)
SALT AND FRESHLY GROUND PEPPER

Slice the endive very thinly. Melt the butter in a deep frying pan, add the endive, mushrooms, and lemon juice, and cook over low heat for 5 minutes, stirring every minute. Add a pinch of sugar and cook for 2 minutes longer, then pour in the champagne. Let it bubble for a moment, and finally add the cream. Cook over medium heat until the coulis has reduced by half. Purée in a blender for 5 minutes, then pass through a conical sieve. Season with salt and pepper and add the truffle if you wish. Keep the coulis warm, and serve it within 10 minutes of blending.

Leek Coulis with Curry

Coulis de poireaux au curry

Spread a spoonful of this coulis over individual plates and top with grilled or pan-fried firm-fleshed fish such as monkfish or turbot, or some shrimp à la meunière.

Serves 8
PREPARATION TIME: 10 MINUTES
COOKING TIME: ABOUT 40 MINUTES

Ingredients:
1 POUND TENDER SMALL OR MEDIUM LEEKS
3 TABLESPOONS BUTTER
$1/2$ TEASPOON CURRY POWDER
1 CUP CHICKEN STOCK (PAGE 18)
$1 1/4$ CUPS HEAVY CREAM
$1/2$ TEASPOON MUSTARD POWDER
SALT AND FRESHLY GROUND PEPPER

Cut off the greenest parts of the leeks and the root ends. Split the leeks lengthwise, wash meticulously in cold water, and slice them finely. Blanch in boiling salted water, refresh, and drain.

In a thick-bottomed saucepan, melt the butter and sweat the leeks gently for 10 minutes. Add the curry powder, then the chicken stock and cook over medium heat for 10 minutes. Add the cream and mustard powder and simmer for 10 minutes longer, then whizz in a blender for 5 minutes. Pass the coulis through a conical sieve back into the pan. Season and keep the coulis warm, without letting it boil, until ready to serve.

Morel Coulis

Coulis de morilles

Truly one for mushroom lovers, this coulis is excellent served with pan-fried medallions of veal or fresh pasta — make a well in the middle of the pasta and pour in the coulis. You can substitute button mushrooms for the morels, but of course the flavor will not be as fine.

Serves 8
PREPARATION TIME: 10 MINUTES
COOKING TIME: ABOUT 25 MINUTES

Ingredients:
3 TABLESPOONS BUTTER
$1/3$ CUP CHOPPED SHALLOT
$1/2$ POUND FRESH MORELS, FINELY SLICED, OR
3 OUNCES DRIED MORELS, REHYDRATED IN
BOILING WATER FOR 10 MINUTES,
THEN FINELY SLICED
$1 1/4$ CUPS CHICKEN STOCK (PAGE 18)
$1 1/2$ CUPS HEAVY CREAM
2 OUNCES COOKED OR CANNED DUCK OR
GOOSE FOIE GRAS
SALT AND FRESHLY GROUND PEPPER

Melt the butter in a thick-bottomed saucepan. Add the shallot, then the morels and sweat gently for 5 minutes. Add the chicken stock and cook over medium heat for 5 minutes. Next add the cream and, still over medium heat, reduce the coulis by one-third, stirring occasionally with a wooden spoon. Transfer to a blender and process for 5 minutes.

Pass the coulis through a conical sieve back into the saucepan, set over low heat, and whisk in the foie gras, a small piece at a time. Season the coulis with salt and pepper and serve immediately or, if necessary, keep it warm on a very low heat for a few minutes.

2 3

4 5

Parsley Coulis

Coulis de persil

This coulis is delicious served in little ramekins or egg coddlers, topped with a few snails sautéed in browned butter. When serving the coulis with a grilled veal chop, I sometimes substitute a pinch of curry powder for the pepper.

Serves 8
PREPARATION TIME: 10 MINUTES
COOKING TIME: 8–10 MINUTES

Ingredients:
9 CUPS CURLY OR FLAT-LEAF PARSLEY, STEMS
REMOVED
1 1/4 CUPS HEAVY CREAM
1/3 CUP THINLY SLICED SHALLOTS
1/2 CUP MILK, AT BOILING POINT
SALT AND FRESHLY GROUND PEPPER

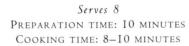

Wash the parsley in plenty of cold water (1). Bring a pan of lightly salted water to a boil and plunge in the parsley (2). Boil for 2 minutes, then refresh in ice water (3). Drain, put the parsley in a cloth (4), and squeeze the parsley to eliminate all the water (5).

In a saucepan, boil the cream with the shallot and reduce by one-third. Add the parsley (6) and bubble for 2 minutes, stirring continuously with a wooden spoon. Take the pan off the heat, add the boiling milk, and stir. Purée in a blender for 2–3 minutes, until very smooth, then rub through a drum sieve (7), using a plastic scraper. Season with salt and pepper. Serve hot, but do not boil the coulis once it has been sieved.

PARSLEY COULIS
TOPPED WITH SNAILS
SAUTÉED IN BROWNED
BUTTER

CHAPTER 5

All terrines and pâtés — pork, veal, poultry, or game — are improved and enhanced by the addition of a sauce or chutney, which is often fruity and refreshing, with a hint of acidity. Such sauces help to develop the flavor of the meats.

Sauces & Chutneys for Terrines, Pâtés & Game

My own favorite is Cumberland sauce; we often serve it at The Waterside Inn and I never tire of it. At home, I always keep a few jars of pear or peach chutney, which I love to eat with leftover cold roast pheasant or partridge. Most of these sauces are simple to prepare and taste wonderful served with all pâtés and terrines, whether homemade or bought from a specialty food shop.

Hot game sauces fill the kitchen with heavenly aromas as they cook. They help to make high or very rich game more digestible. Among my favorites is that all-time great, poivrade sauce, whose satisfying flavor marries well with almost all game. The glowing autumnal colors and fruity flavors of sauces made with figs or port wine will awaken your appetite. You will also discover that bitter chocolate strays from the confines of desserts into one of these savory sauces.

ROAST PARTRIDGE WITH
PORT-WINE SAUCE AND
APPLE SAUCE

Port-Wine Sauce

Sauce au porto

One of my favorite simple game dishes is pan-fried pheasant breasts served with this light sauce. It is also excellent with pan-fried venison chops and roast partridge. For preference, I would use black currants, but since their season is short, I also use cranberries. These give the sauce a very slightly bitter tinge that is refreshing and very digestible.

Serves 4
PREPARATION TIME: 10 MINUTES
COOKING TIME: 30 MINUTES

Ingredients:
4 TABLESPOONS BUTTER
1/2 CUP VERY FINELY SLICED SHALLOTS
1 1/3 CUPS FINELY SLICED BUTTON MUSHROOMS
1/2 CUP CRANBERRIES OR BLACK CURRANTS
1 CUP RED PORT WINE, AT LEAST 10 YEARS OLD
DRIED ZEST OF 1/4 ORANGE
1 1/4 CUPS VEAL STOCK (PAGE 16)
OR GAME STOCK (PAGE 19)
SALT AND FRESHLY GROUND PEPPER

Melt half the butter in a small saucepan. Add the shallots and sweat until soft, then add the mushrooms and cranberries or black currants and cook gently for 3–4 minutes. Pour in the port, add the orange zest, and reduce by one-third. Add the stock and simmer for 25 minutes, skimming the surface whenever necessary.

Pass the sauce through a conical sieve, swirl in the rest of the butter, shaking and rotating the pan, and then season to taste with salt and pepper.

(Picture page 72)

Apple Sauce

Sauce aux pommes

Apple sauce is delicious served with young wild boar, wild duck, roast partridge and pheasant, or roast pork.

Serves 6
PREPARATION TIME: 5 MINUTES
COOKING TIME: ABOUT 15 MINUTES

Ingredients:
1 POUND APPLES, PREFERABLY PIPPINS
2/3 CUP WATER
1 1/2 TABLESPOONS SUGAR
JUICE OF 1/2 LEMON
1/2 CINNAMON STICK, OR A PINCH OF GROUND CINNAMON
2 TABLESPOONS BUTTER
A PINCH OF SALT

Peel and core the apples and dice them finely. Place in a thick-bottomed saucepan together with all the other ingredients except the butter and salt. Set over medium heat, cover, and cook for about 15 minutes, until the apples are tender but not dried out. Take the pan off the heat and, with a small whisk, whisk in the butter and a pinch of salt to make a very smooth compote. The consistency of the sauce will vary according to how ripe or green the apples are. If it seems too thick, add a tablespoon of water. Remove the cinnamon stick before serving.

(Picture page 72)

Marinated Cucumber Relish

Concombre mariné au vinaigre

I really enjoy this cucumber relish, which our young protégé Mark Prescott often serves at his pub, The White Hart at Nayland. It is delicious served with fish galantines and terrines or with gravlax.

Makes 1¼ pounds
PREPARATION TIME: ABOUT 10 MINUTES,
PLUS 2 HOURS' MARINATING
COOKING TIME: ABOUT 1 HOUR 30 MINUTES

Ingredients:
For the marinated cucumbers
(prepare these 2 hours in advance)
2¼ POUNDS ENGLISH HOTHOUSE CUCUMBERS
1 CUP THINLY SLICED ONIONS
1 GREEN BELL PEPPER
1 RED BELL PEPPER
1 RED CHILI PEPPER
SALT

For the syrup:
2 CUPS WHITE WINE
1½ CUPS LIGHT BROWN SUGAR
A SMALL PINCH OF GROUND CLOVES
1 TEASPOON TURMERIC
2 TEASPOONS MUSTARD SEEDS
1 TEASPOON FENNEL SEEDS

Prepare and marinate the cucumbers 2 hours in advance. Leave them unpeeled, but halve them lengthwise, scoop out the seeds, and slice the flesh very thinly. Peel the green and red bell peppers, remove the seeds and white membranes, and cut the flesh into very fine *julienne*. Cut the chili into very fine *julienne*. Put all the prepared vegetables, including the onions, in a non-metallic bowl, add salt to taste, and leave to marinate for 2 hours.

To make the syrup, put all the ingredients in a saucepan and bring slowly to a boil over low heat. Cook for about 45 minutes, until the syrup is thick enough to coat a wooden spoon and your finger leaves a clear trace when you run it down the spoon.

Drain the marinated ingredients, press to eliminate as much liquid as possible, and add them to the syrup. Cook gently for 45 minutes, stirring occasionally with a wooden spoon, until the relish has a soft, melting, jam-like consistency. Transfer it to an airtight jar and keep in a cool place until ready to use. It will keep in the refrigerator for several weeks.

Poivrade Sauce

Sauce poivrade

This sauce should be made with the marinade you have used for the game the sauce is to accompany. Poivrade sauce is rich and powerful and perfect for a large piece of game, such as a leg of venison, saddle of young wild boar, or roast hare or rabbit. It can also be served with pan-fried noisettes of venison. As these are delicate, you should not overwhelm the flavor with a very full-bodied sauce, so use only half the given quantity of marinade and do not reduce the sauce too much.

Serves 6
PREPARATION TIME: 20 MINUTES
COOKING TIME: ABOUT I HOUR 15 MINUTES

Ingredients:
3 TABLESPOONS OIL
I POUND TRIMMINGS OF FURRED GAME (E.G.
VENISON, WILD BOAR), CUT IN PIECES
I CUP CHOPPED CARROTS
$1/2$ CUP CHOPPED ONION
2 TABLESPOONS RED WINE VINEGAR
$7/8$ CUP COOKED MARINADE (PAGE 23)
2 CUPS VEAL STOCK (PAGE 16)
OR GAME STOCK (PAGE 19)
I BOUQUET GARNI (PAGE 10)
6 PEPPERCORNS, CRUSHED
3 TABLESPOONS BUTTER, CHILLED AND DICED
SALT AND FRESHLY GROUND PEPPER

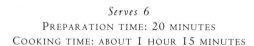

Heat the oil in a deep frying pan, put in the game trimmings (1), and brown them over high heat (2). Strain off the oil and fat released by the cooking, add the chopped carrot and onion to the pan, and sweat over low heat for 3 minutes (3). Pour in the vinegar and marinade and cook over medium heat for 5 minutes (4). Add the stock and bouquet garni and cook at a bare simmer for 45 minutes (5), then add the crushed peppercorns and cook for 10 minutes longer.

Strain the sauce through a conical sieve into a small saucepan. Off the heat, swirl in the butter, a little at a time (6), until the sauce is smooth and glossy (7). Season to taste and serve at once, or keep the sauce warm, taking care not to let it boil. If you are going to do this, add the butter only at the last moment.

GRAND VENEUR SAUCE: Add 2 teaspoons red-currant jelly and 2 tablespoons heavy cream to the poivrade sauce to make a Grand Veneur Sauce (this means "Master of the King's Hunt").

Cumberland Sauce

Sauce Cumberland

This sauce miraculously enhances the character of meats and terrines. Serve it cold with galantines and ballotines, pork pies, or any poultry or game. The sauce tastes even better the day after it is made.

Serves 4
PREPARATION TIME: 10 MINUTES
COOKING TIME: 20 MINUTES

Ingredients:
1 MEDIUM SHALLOT, MINCED
$^1/_4$ CUP WINE VINEGAR, PREFERABLY RED
12 WHITE PEPPERCORNS, CRUSHED
$^1/_2$ CUP VEAL STOCK (PAGE 16)
$^1/_4$ CUP RUBY PORT WINE
2 TABLESPOONS RED-CURRANT JELLY
1 TEASPOON WORCESTERSHIRE SAUCE
JUICE OF 1 ORANGE
ZEST OF 1 LEMON, BLANCHED AND
CUT IN JULIENNE
SALT

COMBINE THE VINEGAR, SHALLOT, AND PEPPERCORNS, AND REDUCE BY TWO-THIRDS

Combine the shallot, vinegar, and peppercorns in a small saucepan and reduce by two-thirds over high heat. Add the veal stock, port, red-currant jelly, Worcestershire sauce, and orange juice, and quickly bring to a boil, then lower the heat and simmer gently for 20 minutes. Season with salt.

Pass the sauce through a conical strainer into a bowl. Cool and then refrigerate, as the sauce should be served very cold. Just before serving, stir in the *julienne* of lemon zest.

SHRED THE BLANCHED LEMON ZEST INTO JULIENNE

CUMBERLAND SAUCE TASTES WONDERFUL WITH ALL MEAT AND GAME TERRINES

LEFT: ADD THE PORT WINE TO THE SAUCE

Rich Pomerol Sauce

Sauce riche au vin de Pomerol

This rich, intense, and complex sauce is perfect with a well-marinated roast gigot of young wild boar. The perfect accompaniments to such a regal game dish are spätzle noodles, chestnuts, and braised celeriac.

Serves 6
PREPARATION TIME: 10 MINUTES
COOKING TIME: ABOUT 25 MINUTES

Ingredients:
1 1/4 CUPS TOP QUALITY POMEROL WINE
1 QUANTITY POIVRADE SAUCE (PAGE 76), WITHOUT THE ADDED BUTTER
3/4 OUNCE UNSWEETENED CHOCOLATE, MELTED
5 TABLESPOONS FOIE-GRAS BUTTER (PAGE 63)
SALT AND FRESHLY GROUND PEPPER

Pour the wine into a saucepan and reduce it by one-third. Add the poivrade sauce and simmer gently for 15 minutes, then whisk in the melted chocolate. Bubble the sauce for 30 seconds, then remove from the heat and whisk in the foie-gras butter, a little at a time. Pass the sauce through a wire-mesh conical sieve, season with salt and pepper, and serve at once.

Pumpkin Sauce with Sweet Spices

Sauce au potiron et aux épices douces

This fruity sauce, with its delicate flavor of spices, is perfect with fillets of wild rabbit, noisettes of young wild boar, or pan-fried breast of wild duck served with a light garlic-flavored potato purée and crisply cooked snow peas.

Serves 4
PREPARATION TIME: 20 MINUTES
COOKING TIME: ABOUT 1 1/2 HOURS

Ingredients:
3 TABLESPOONS OIL
1 POUND GAME TRIMMINGS OR CHOPPED GAME CARCASSES
1/2 CUP MINCED SHALLOTS
2 1/2 CUPS PUMPKIN FLESH CUT IN SMALL CUBES
1/4 CUP RASPBERRY VINEGAR, HOMEMADE (PAGE 44) OR STORE-BOUGHT
7/8 CUP SWEET WHITE WINE (SAUTERNES OR BARSAC)
2 CUPS VEGETABLE STOCK (PAGE 22)
1 BOUQUET GARNI (PAGE 10)
1 VANILLA BEAN, SPLIT LENGTHWISE
3 STAR ANISE
1 1/2 TABLESPOONS BUTTER, CHILLED AND DICED
SALT AND FRESHLY GROUND PEPPER

Heat the oil in a deep frying pan, add the game trimmings or carcasses, and briskly brown them all over. Pour off the oil and fat released by the game, then put in the shallots and pumpkin and sweat them gently over low heat for 3 minutes. Remove from the heat and add the raspberry vinegar. After 1 minute, deglaze with the white wine and simmer for 5 minutes. Add the vegetable stock, bouquet garni, vanilla, and star anise and cook very gently for 45 minutes, skimming the surface whenever necessary.

Pass the sauce through a wire-mesh conical sieve into a clean pan and reduce until it coats the back of a spoon. Off the heat, whisk in the butter, a little at a time. Season to taste with salt and pepper, and serve the sauce at once.

Arabica Fig Sauce

Sauces aux figues arabica

This sauce is excellent with roast wild duck or squab. Fresh figs poached in red wine make a wonderful garnish. Be careful not to boil the sauce after adding the coffee, or it will become slightly bitter.

Serves 8
PREPARATION TIME: 10 MINUTES
COOKING TIME: ABOUT 40 MINUTES

Ingredients:
6 VERY RIPE FRESH FIGS, EACH
CUT IN 6 PIECES
$^1/_2$ CUP RUBY PORT WINE
1$^3/_4$ CUPS GAME STOCK (PAGE 19)
6 BLACK PEPPERCORNS, CRUSHED
1 TABLESPOON INSTANT COFFEE POWDER, DISSOLVED
IN 1 TABLESPOON WATER
3 TABLESPOONS BUTTER, CHILLED AND DICED
SALT AND FRESHLY GROUND PEPPER

Put the figs and port wine in a saucepan and simmer gently for 5 minutes. Pour in the game stock, add the crushed peppercorns, and bubble gently for 25 minutes, skimming the surface from time to time. Add the coffee, then immediately remove from the heat.

Pour the sauce into a blender, whizz for 30 seconds, then pass it through a wire-mesh conical sieve. Whisk in the butter, one piece at a time. Season to taste with salt and pepper, and serve immediately.

Peach Chutney

Chutney aux pêches

Make this chutney in summer, when peaches are fresh and cheap. It is delicious served with terrines and pâtés, cold cuts, and especially with cold chicken for a picnic.

Makes about 1$^1/_2$ pounds
PREPARATION TIME: 25 MINUTES
COOKING TIME: ABOUT 1 HOUR 10 MINUTES

Ingredients:
$^1/_2$ CUP PEELED, GRATED APPLE
$^1/_2$ TEASPOON SALT
$^1/_2$ CUP CHOPPED VERY RIPE TOMATOES, PEELED AND
SEEDED
$^1/_3$ CUP MINCED ONION
ZEST OF 1 LIME, MINCED
JUICE OF 1 LIME
$^3/_4$ CUP SUGAR
$^1/_2$ TEASPOON GROUND CINNAMON
$^1/_2$ TEASPOON GROUND NUTMEG
$^1/_2$ TEASPOON GROUND WHITE PEPPER
1 GARLIC CLOVE, CRUSHED
1 TABLESPOON MINCED FRESH GINGER
$^2/_3$ CUP WHITE WINE VINEGAR
$^3/_4$ CUP SLICED ALMONDS
1 POUND PEACHES, PREFERABLY YELLOW, PEELED,
PITTED, AND ROUGHLY CUT IN LARGE DICE

Combine all the ingredients except the peaches in a thick-bottomed saucepan and bring to a boil over very low heat, stirring from time to time with a wooden spoon. Continue to cook for about 30 minutes, giving a stir every 10 minutes, until the mixture is jam-like and syrupy. Test by wiping your finger down the back of the spoon; it should leave a clear trace.

Add the peaches and cook very gently for 40 minutes longer, stirring every 10 minutes. Transfer the chutney to a canning jar and leave to cool completely, then seal the jar. Keep in the refrigerator until needed (it will keep for several weeks).

INGREDIENTS FOR PEAR
CHUTNEY

BOIL ALL THE INGREDIENTS
EXCEPT THE PEARS FOR
ABOUT 1 HOUR

THE MIXTURE SHOULD
HAVE THE CONSISTENCY
OF JAM

Pear Chutney

Chutney aux poires

This chutney is best left for a few days before you eat it. Serve it with cold cuts, terrines, pâtés, and game, or simply spread on a slice of toast.

Makes about 1 1/4 pounds
PREPARATION TIME: 30 MINUTES
COOKING TIME: ABOUT 1 HOUR 50 MINUTES

Ingredients:
1/2 CUP PEELED, GRATED APPLE
1/2 TEASPOON SALT
1/2 CUP CHOPPED VERY RIPE TOMATOES, PEELED AND
SEEDED
1/3 CUP MINCED ONION
1/3 CUP GOLDEN RAISINS
1 TABLESPOON COARSELY CHOPPED ORANGE ZEST
JUICE OF 1 ORANGE
3/4 CUP SUGAR
1/4 TEASPOON GROUND CINNAMON
1/4 TEASPOON GROUND NUTMEG
1/4 TEASPOON CAYENNE
1 1/2 TABLESPOONS MINCED FRESH GINGER
2/3 CUP WHITE WINE VINEGAR
A PINCH OF SAFFRON POWDER OR THREADS
3/4 POUND PEARS, PEELED, CORED, AND CUT IN
LARGE DICE

Combine all the ingredients except the pears in a thick-bottomed saucepan and bring to a boil over very low heat, stirring from time to time with a wooden spoon. Continue to cook for about 1 hour, giving a stir every 10 minutes, until the mixture is jam-like and syrupy. Test by wiping your finger down the back of the spoon; it should leave a clear trace.

Add the pears and cook very gently for 40 minutes longer, stirring every 10 minutes. Transfer the chutney to a canning jar and leave to cool completely, then seal the jar. Keep in the refrigerator until needed (it will keep for several weeks).

ADD THE PEARS TO THE
MIXTURE

COOK THE CHUTNEY FOR 40
MINUTES LONGER, STIRRING
EVERY 10 MINUTES

RIGHT: USE A FUNNEL TO
TRANSFER THE CHUTNEY TO
A CANNING JAR

Venison Sauce with Blackberries

Sauce chevreuil aux mûres

This fragrant, satisfying, but not overly-rich sauce is ideal with a roast saddle or gigot of venison, especially in the fall and winter months.

Serves 6
PREPARATION TIME: 10 MINUTES
COOKING TIME: ABOUT 40 MINUTES

Ingredients:
I CUP BLACKBERRIES
2$^{1}/_{2}$ TABLESPOONS SUGAR
2 TABLESPOONS RED WINE VINEGAR
2$^{1}/_{2}$ CUPS GAME STOCK (PAGE 19)
DRIED ZEST OF $^{1}/_{2}$ ORANGE
$^{1}/_{2}$ CINNAMON STICK
$^{1}/_{4}$ CUP BANYULS WINE
4 TABLESPOONS BUTTER, WELL CHILLED AND DICED
SALT AND FRESHLY GROUND PEPPER

Put the blackberries and sugar in a saucepan and cook over low heat, stirring with a wooden spoon, until the blackberries have collapsed into a purée. Remove from the heat, add the vinegar, and give a stir, then pour in the game stock. Add the dried orange zest and cinnamon, bring to a boil, and simmer gently for 25 minutes, skimming the surface whenever necessary. Add the wine and cook for 5 minutes longer, then pass the sauce through a wire-mesh conical sieve into another saucepan. Whisk in the butter, a little at a time, season the sauce with salt and pepper, and serve at once.

Vineyard Sauce with Five Spices

Sauce vigneronne aux cinque épices

For a delicious main course, serve this sauce with roast pheasant or partridge garnished with peeled and seeded grapes. If you prefer a less pronounced gamey flavor, substitute veal stock for the game stock.

Serves 6
PREPARATION TIME: 15 MINUTES
COOKING TIME: ABOUT 45 MINUTES

Ingredients:
24 GRAPES, PEELED AND SEEDED
$^{1}/_{4}$ CUP SUGAR
$^{1}/_{4}$ CUP ARMAGNAC OR COGNAC
I$^{1}/_{4}$ CUPS RED WINE, PREFERABLY CÔTES DU RHÔNE
2 CUPS GAME STOCK (PAGE 19)
I TEASPOON FIVE-SPICE POWDER
I SMALL BOUQUET GARNI (PAGE 10),
INCLUDING 2 SAGE LEAVES
4 TABLESPOONS BUTTER, CHILLED AND DICED
SALT AND FRESHLY GROUND PEPPER

Put the grapes and sugar in a saucepan, set over medium heat, and cook, stirring every minute with a wooden spoon, until the grapes have disintegrated into a lightly caramelized compote. Add the Armagnac or cognac and ignite it, then pour in the wine and cook until it has reduced by one-third.

Add all the other ingredients and simmer for 30 minutes, or until the sauce is thick enough to coat the back of a spoon, skimming the surface whenever necessary. Pass the sauce through a wire-mesh conical sieve, season with salt and pepper, and whisk in the chilled butter, a little at a time. Serve immediately.

Quick Sauce for Game Birds

Sauce minute pour gibier à plumes

This quickly prepared but serious sauce is not too robust; however, since it absorbs the savor of the carcasses during its brief cooking, it retains the full flavor of the game birds.

Serves 4
PREPARATION TIME: 5 MINUTES
COOKING TIME: ABOUT 30 MINUTES

Ingredients:
2 WILD DUCK, OR 2 SNIPE, OR 4 SQUAB
$^1/_4$ CUP COGNAC OR ARMAGNAC
$^2/_3$ CUP RED WINE
2 CUPS VEGETABLE STOCK (PAGE 22)
5 JUNIPER BERRIES, CRUSHED
I SPRIG OF THYME
$^1/_2$ BAY LEAF
$^1/_4$ CUP HEAVY CREAM
SALT AND FRESHLY GROUND PEPPER

Roast the game birds until they are cooked to your liking, then remove the thighs and breasts, wrap them in foil, and keep them warm until ready to eat.

Chop the carcasses, place in a saucepan, and heat them through, then add the Armagnac or cognac and ignite it. Pour in the red wine and reduce it by half over high heat, then add the vegetable stock, juniper berries, thyme, and bay leaf. Cook briskly to reduce the liquid by half. Add the cream and bubble for 3 minutes longer. Pass the sauce through a wire-mesh conical sieve, season with salt and pepper, and serve immediately with the reserved breast and thigh meat.

Cranberry and Bilberry Sauce

Sauce aux airelles et myrtilles

I serve this sauce with terrines of game or pâtés en croûte. It is also good served just warm with wild roast goose. The berries, particularly bilberries, can sometimes be rather tart; if so, add about $2^1/_2$ tablespoons sugar to the sauce halfway through cooking (you won't need this if you are using blueberries).

Serves 8
PREPARATION TIME: 5 MINUTES
COOKING TIME: ABOUT 30 MINUTES

Ingredients:
I $^1/_2$ CUPS CRANBERRIES
I CUP COLD WATER
6 TABLESPOONS SUGAR
I CLOVE, CRUSHED
I CUP FRESH BILBERRIES OR BLUEBERRIES
JUICE OF I LEMON
ZEST OF I LEMON, CUT IN
JULIENNE AND BLANCHED

Put the cranberries in a saucepan, add $^1/_2$ cup cold water, the sugar, and clove, and cook gently for 10 minutes. Add the bilberries, the remaining cold water, and the lemon juice and simmer for 20 minutes. Keep the sauce at room temperature; it should not be served too cold. If you prefer a very smooth sauce with no fruit skins, pass it through a strainer. Stir in the lemon zest just before serving.

CHAPTER 6

These sauces should be delicate and light; their flavor should harmonize with the seafood they accompany and never dominate it. This is particularly important in the case of white fish.

Sauces for Fish & Shellfish

I like to serve fish with a nage, a light, aromatic stock, to which I sometimes add just a tiny soupçon of fresh herbs, like snipped chervil, basil, or tarragon. I prefer my fish barely cooked, so that it remains juicy. The sauce should be there to bring out the fresh, salty tang and the delicate flavor of the sea, adding extra pleasure to the palate.

In contrast, sauces for crustaceans and mollusks should be flavored with stronger herbs and spices to give them a more defined edge and character.

Sauces for fish and seafood often contain dry white wine; variations include beer, champagne, vermouth, or even a sweet Sauternes.

TAGLIATELLE AND SEAFOOD SAUCE
WITH SAFFRON

Seafood Sauce with Saffron

Sauce aux fruits de mer safranée

This is the perfect sauce for any lightly poached seafood, for jumbo shrimp or lobster, or for fresh flat pasta.

Serves 4
PREPARATION TIME: 10 MINUTES
COOKING TIME: ABOUT 20 MINUTES

Ingredients:
1½ CUPS COOKING JUICES FROM SHELLFISH, SUCH
AS MUSSELS, SCALLOPS, OYSTERS, CLAMS, ETC
1 CUP FISH STOCK (PAGE 21), OR COOKING JUICES
FROM SHRIMP OR LOBSTER
A PINCH OF SAFFRON THREADS
1 CUP HEAVY CREAM
SALT AND FRESHLY GROUND WHITE PEPPER

Combine the shellfish juices and fish stock in a saucepan, set over high heat, and reduce by two-thirds. Add the saffron and cream and bubble for 5 minutes, until the sauce will lightly coat the back of a spoon. Pass it through a conical sieve and season to taste.

For a less calorific sauce, you can substitute fromage blanc for the heavy cream, but do not allow the sauce to boil. Heat it to 195°F and whisk well before serving, or, better still, give it a quick whizz in a blender.

(Picture page 86)

Red-Wine Sauce

Sauce lie de vin

This vinous, characterful sauce is traditionally made with the dregs or "lees" at the bottom of the bottle. Serve it as a base for pink-fleshed fish, such as thin slices (scallops) of salmon or tuna. Pan-fry the fish at the last moment, pour the sauce onto the plate, and place the fish on top.

Serves 8
PREPARATION TIME: 5 MINUTES
COOKING TIME: ABOUT 40 MINUTES

Ingredients:
1¼ CUPS FULL-BODIED RED WINE,
PREFERABLY BORDEAUX
⅞ CUP VEAL STOCK (PAGE 16)
1¼ CUPS FISH STOCK (PAGE 21), MADE
WITH RED WINE
⅓ CUP FINELY SLICED SHALLOTS
¾ CUP FINELY SLICED BUTTON MUSHROOMS
1 SMALL BOUQUET GARNI (PAGE 10)
¼ CUP HEAVY CREAM
14 TABLESPOONS BUTTER, CHILLED AND DICED
SALT AND FRESHLY GROUND PEPPER

Combine all the ingredients except the cream and butter in a saucepan, set over medium heat, and reduce until slightly syrupy. Remove the bouquet garni, add the cream, and give the sauce a good bubble, then strain it through a conical sieve into a clean saucepan. Whisk in the butter, a small piece at a time, until the sauce is rich and glossy. Season to taste and serve hot.

Nantua Sauce

Sauce Nantua

An excellent sauce for large shrimp, scallops, and any white fish with delicate, firm flesh. A tablespoon of snipped tarragon added just before serving will make the sauce taste even better.

Serves 8
PREPARATION TIME: 20 MINUTES
COOKING TIME: ABOUT 50 MINUTES

Ingredients:
1/2 CUP BUTTER
1/2 CUP VERY FINELY SLICED SHALLOTS
3/4 CUP VERY FINELY SLICED BUTTON MUSHROOMS
16 CRAYFISH OR *LANGOUSTINE* (DUBLIN BAY PRAWN)
HEADS, RAW OR COOKED, ROUGHLY CHOPPED
2 TABLESPOONS COGNAC
2/3 CUP DRY WHITE WINE
1 1/4 CUPS FISH STOCK (PAGE 21)
1 SMALL BOUQUET GARNI (PAGE 10), INCLUDING A
SPRIG OR 2 OF TARRAGON
1/2 CUP CHOPPED RIPE TOMATOES, PEELED AND
SEEDED
A PINCH OF CAYENNE
1 1/4 CUPS HEAVY CREAM
SALT AND FRESHLY GROUND PEPPER

In a shallow saucepan, melt 3 tablespoons butter over low heat. Add the shallots and mushrooms and sweat for 1 minute. Add the crayfish or prawn heads to the pan, increase the heat, and fry briskly for 2–3 minutes, stirring continuously with a spatula.

Pour in the cognac, and ignite with a match. Add the wine and reduce by half, then pour in the fish stock. Bring to a boil, then lower the heat so that the sauce bubbles gently. Add the bouquet garni, tomatoes, cayenne, and a bit of salt and cook for 30 minutes.

Stir in the cream and bubble the sauce for 10 minutes longer. Remove the bouquet garni, transfer the contents of the pan to a food processor, and whizz for 2 minutes. Strain the sauce through a fine-mesh conical sieve into a clean saucepan, rubbing it through with the back of a ladle. Bring the sauce back to a boil and season with salt and pepper. Off the heat, whisk in the remaining butter, a little at a time, until the sauce is smooth and glossy. It is now ready to serve.

Champagne Sauce

Sauce Champagne

This sauce is perfect for poached white fish, such as John Dory, turbot, or sole. You can, of course, substitute a good sparkling white wine for French champagne.

Serves 8
PREPARATION TIME: 10 MINUTES
COOKING TIME: ABOUT 50 MINUTES

Ingredients:
4 TABLESPOONS BUTTER
1/2 CUP VERY FINELY SLICED SHALLOTS
3/4 CUP FINELY SLICED BUTTON MUSHROOMS
1 3/4 CUPS BRUT CHAMPAGNE
1 1/4 CUPS FISH STOCK (PAGE 21)
2 CUPS HEAVY CREAM
SALT AND FRESHLY GROUND WHITE PEPPER

In a saucepan, melt 1 1/2 tablespoons butter. Add the shallots and sweat them for 1 minute, without coloring. Add the mushrooms and cook for 2 minutes longer, stirring continuously with a wooden spatula. Pour in the champagne and reduce by one-third over medium heat. Add the fish stock and reduce the sauce by half.

Pour in the cream and reduce the sauce until it lightly coats the back of a spoon. Pass it through a fine-mesh conical sieve into a clean pan. Whisk in the remaining butter, a little at a time, then season the sauce with salt and pepper.

For a lighter texture, whizz the sauce in a food processor for 1 minute before serving.

Américaine Sauce

Sauce américaine

This classic "star" sauce should be eaten with a spoon. It takes time to prepare, but is worth the effort. Serve it with firm-fleshed fish, such as poached turbot, or a turbot soufflé homardine.

Serves 6
PREPARATION TIME: 40 MINUTES
COOKING TIME: ABOUT 1 HOUR

Ingredients:
1 LIVE LOBSTER, 1 3/4-2 POUNDS
A SMALL PINCH OF CAYENNE
1/2 CUP PEANUT OIL
1/3 CUP VERY FINELY DICED CARROTS
3 TABLESPOONS VERY FINELY DICED SHALLOT OR ONION
2 GARLIC CLOVES, UNPEELED AND CRUSHED
1/4 CUP COGNAC OR ARMAGNAC
1 1/4 CUPS DRY WHITE WINE
1 1/4 CUPS FISH STOCK (PAGE 21)
1/2 POUND VERY RIPE TOMATOES, PEELED, SEEDED, AND CHOPPED (1 1/2 CUPS)
1 BOUQUET GARNI (PAGE 10), CONTAINING A SPRIG OF TARRAGON
4 1/2 TABLESPOONS BUTTER
1 1/2 TABLESPOONS FLOUR
1/3 CUP HEAVY CREAM (OPTIONAL)
SALT AND FRESHLY GROUND PEPPER

Bring a large pan of water to a boil. Rinse the lobster under cold running water and plunge it into the boiling water for 45 seconds. Separate the head and body, and cut the claw joints and tail into rings across the articulations. Split the head lengthwise and remove the gritty sac close to the feelers, and the dirty white membranes. Scrape out the greenish coral (tomalley) from inside the head and reserve in a bowl. Season the lobster with cayenne, salt, and pepper.

In a deep frying pan or shallow saucepan, heat the oil over high heat. As soon as it is sizzling hot, add all the lobster pieces (1) and sauté until the shell turns bright red and the flesh is lightly colored (2). Remove the lobster pieces with a slotted spoon and place on a plate. Discard most of the cooking oil.

Using the same pan, sweat the carrot and shallot until soft but not colored. Add the garlic (3), return the lobster pieces to the pan, pour in the cognac (4),

ABOVE AND BELOW: SEPARATE THE HEAD AND THE BODY, AND CUT THE CLAW JOINTS AND TAIL IN RINGS

SPLIT THE HEAD AND REMOVE THE GRITTY SAC

SCRAPE OUT THE GREENISH CORAL FROM INSIDE THE HEAD AND RESERVE

REMOVE THE
LOBSTER CLAWS
AND TAILS AND
RESERVE

and light with a match. Add the wine and fish stock, then add the tomatoes, bouquet garni, and a touch of salt. As soon as the mixture comes to a boil, lower the heat and cook gently for 15 minutes. Remove and reserve the claws and rings of lobster tail containing the meat. Cook the sauce at a gentle bubble for a further 30 minutes, skimming it every 15 minutes.

Using a fork, mash together the reserved lobster coral, butter, and flour, and add this mixture to the sauce, a little at a time. Cook for 5 minutes longer, then add the cream if desired and pass the sauce through a fine-mesh conical strainer, pressing it through with the the back of a ladle. Season with salt and pepper. For a lighter texture, whizz the sauce in a food processor for 1 minute. Remove the reserved lobster meat from the shell, dice it and add to the sauce just before serving.

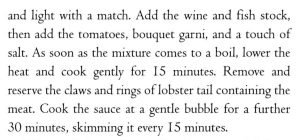

ADD THE CREAM
(OPTIONAL)

ADD THE LOBSTER
CORAL, BUTTER, AND
FLOUR MIXTURE

RIGHT: PASS THE SAUCE
THROUGH A SIEVE, PRESSING
WITH THE BACK OF A LADLE

92

Thermidor Sauce

Sauce thermidor

This famous companion to lobster thermidor is sadly often poorly made and therefore disappointing. I enjoy it with almost all shellfish, especially mixed with crabmeat and served au gratin. *If you wish, add a teaspoon of cognac to the sauce at the end of cooking.*

Serves 6
PREPARATION TIME: 10 MINUTES
COOKING TIME: ABOUT 40 MINUTES

Ingredients:
1/3 CUP MINCED SHALLOTS
1 CUP FISH STOCK (PAGE 21)
1 CUP DRY WHITE WINE
1 1/4 CUPS BÉCHAMEL SAUCE (PAGE 128)
1/2 CUP HEAVY CREAM
1 TEASPOON STRONG DIJON MUSTARD
1 TEASPOON ENGLISH MUSTARD POWDER, DISSOLVED
IN A FEW DROPS OF WATER
4 TABLESPOONS BUTTER, CHILLED AND DICED
1 TABLESPOON FINELY SNIPPED TARRAGON
SALT AND CAYENNE

Combine the shallots, fish stock, and wine in a saucepan and reduce the liquid by two-thirds. Add the béchamel and cook the sauce over low heat for 20 minutes, stirring every 5 minutes. Pour in the cream, and bubble for 5 minutes, then add both mustards and cook for 2 minutes longer. Remove from the heat and whisk the butter into the sauce, one piece at a time. Season with salt and a large pinch of cayenne. Finally, add the tarragon and serve immediately.

Mango Sauce

Sauce à la mangue

This refreshing, fruity sauce is perfect for outdoor eating in summer. It is excellent with grilled fish or with crustaceans such as lobster or jumbo shrimp.

Serves 6
PREPARATION TIME: 10 MINUTES
COOKING TIME: ABOUT 40 MINUTES

Ingredients:
1 MANGO, ABOUT 1/2 POUND
1/4 CUP COGNAC OR ARMAGNAC
A SMALL PINCH OF CURRY POWDER
1 TABLESPOON SOFT GREEN PEPPERCORNS, WELL
DRAINED
1 1/4 CUPS FISH STOCK (PAGE 21)
1 CUP HEAVY CREAM
1/2 CUP PLAIN YOGURT
1 TABLESPOON SNIPPED FLAT-LEAF PARSLEY
SALT AND FRESHLY GROUND PEPPER

Using a knife with a fine blade, peel the mango and cut away the flesh from around the pit. Put the flesh in a saucepan with the cognac or Armagnac, curry, and green peppercorns and simmer over low heat for 5 minutes. Pour in the fish stock and bubble gently for 20 minutes. Add the cream and cook for 5 minutes longer, then remove the heat and add the yogurt.

Transfer the sauce to a blender and whizz for 30 seconds, then pass it through a wire-mesh conical sieve and season to taste with salt and pepper. Serve the sauce immediately, or keep it warm (but not too hot) in a *bain-marie.* Stir in the parsley just before serving.

Watercress Sauce

Sauce cressonnière

A tasty sauce to serve with grilled scallops or lightly poached oysters. It is extremely light, almost like a bouillon, and should be eaten with a spoon.

Serves 8
PREPARATION TIME: ABOUT 25 MINUTES
COOKING TIME: ABOUT 25 MINUTES

Ingredients:
JUST UNDER 1 POUND VERY GREEN WATERCRESS
7 TABLESPOONS BUTTER
2 CUPS VEGETABLE STOCK (PAGE 22)
2 TABLESPOONS SOFT GREEN PEPPERCORNS
SALT AND FRESHLY GROUND PEPPER

Cut off and discard most of the watercress stems. In a saucepan, melt 2 tablespoons of the butter. Add the watercress and sweat it over low heat for 3 minutes, stirring continuously with a spatula.

Add the vegetable stock and green peppercorns, increase the heat to high, and cook for 10 minutes. Remove from the heat and leave the sauce to infuse for 10 minutes, then pour it into a food processor and whizz for 2 minutes. Pass the sauce through a fine-mesh conical sieve into a clean saucepan, rubbing it through with the back of a ladle. Reheat until bubbling, then take the pan off the heat and whisk in the remaining butter, a little at a time. Season with salt and pepper.

Tomato Nage

Nage de tomates

This light nage *is perfect with lightly poached shellfish, or grilled fish such as slices of salmon or fillets of sole. It can be enhanced with a little snipped basil added at the last moment. If fresh tomatoes are slightly lacking in flavor, add a teaspoon of tomato paste.*

Serves 8
PREPARATION TIME: 15 MINUTES
COOKING TIME: 25 MINUTES

Ingredients:
3/4 POUND VERY RIPE TOMATOES, PEELED,
SEEDED, AND CHOPPED (2 CUPS)
1/3 CUP FINELY SLICED SHALLOTS
2/3 CUP FINELY SLICED BUTTON MUSHROOMS
1 SPRIG OF THYME
1 BAY LEAF
1 CUP VEGETABLE STOCK (PAGE 22)
A PINCH OF SUGAR
1/4 CUP HEAVY CREAM
1 CUP BUTTER
SALT AND FRESHLY GROUND PEPPER

Combine all the ingredients except the cream and butter in a saucepan and bring to a boil over medium heat. As soon as the mixture starts to bubble, lower the heat and reduce the liquid by two-thirds. Now add the cream and bubble the sauce for 3 minutes. Off the heat, whisk in the butter, a little at a time. Strain the sauce through a fine-mesh conical sieve into a clean saucepan and season to taste. The *nage* is now ready to use.

Shrimp Sauce

Sauce aux crevettes

This is delicious with almost all poached, steamed, or braised fish. I also love it poured over quartered hard-boiled eggs. I sometimes add a couple of tablespoons of dry sherry to the sauce just before serving.

Serves 6

PREPARATION TIME: 15 MINUTES
COOKING TIME: ABOUT 45 MINUTES

Ingredients:
3 TABLESPOONS BLOND ROUX, HOT (PAGE 33)
2½ CUPS FISH STOCK, COOLED (PAGE 21)
I CUP HEAVY CREAM
4 TABLESPOONS SHRIMP BUTTER (PAGE 61)
½ CUP COOKED AND PEELED SMALL
SHRIMP
A PINCH OF CAYENNE
SALT AND FRESHLY GROUND PEPPER

Put the hot roux in a saucepan, set over medium heat, and whisk in the cold fish stock. As soon as it comes to a boil, reduce the heat to very low and cook gently for 30 minutes, whisking every 10 minutes and making sure that the whisk goes right into the bottom of the pan. Use a spoon to remove any skin that forms on this *velouté* as it cooks.

After 30 minutes, add the cream and bubble the sauce for 10 minutes longer. Reduce the heat to the lowest possible (use a heat diffuser if you have one) and whisk in the shrimp butter, a little at a time. Season the sauce with salt and pepper and spice it up with cayenne to taste. Pass it through a wire-mesh conical sieve, then add the shrimp and serve immediately.

Fish Fumet with Tomatoes and Basil

Fumet de poissons à la tomate et au basilic

Steamed fillets of fish with delicate flesh such as John Dory, sole, or bream (porgy) are delicious served in a deep plate, bathed with a ladle of this fat-free, summery fumet, redolent with the aromas of tomatoes and basil. If you wish, sprinkle over some very finely shredded basil.

Serves 6

PREPARATION TIME: 5 MINUTES
COOKING TIME: ABOUT 30 MINUTES

Ingredients:
2½ CUPS FISH STOCK (PAGE 21)

For the clarification:
I POUND VERY RIPE TOMATOES, CHOPPED
I SMALL RED BELL PEPPER, WHITE MEMBRANES AND
SEEDS REMOVED, VERY THINLY SLICED
I HEAPED CUP BASIL, COARSELY CHOPPED
4 EGG WHITES
8 PEPPERCORNS, CRUSHED
SALT AND FRESHLY GROUND PEPPER

Mix the clarification ingredients together very thoroughly. Pour the fish stock into a saucepan and add the clarification mixture. Bring to a boil over medium heat, stirring every 5 minutes with a wooden spoon. As soon as the liquid boils, reduce the heat and bubble very gently for 20 minutes. Pass the clarified *fumet* through a wire-mesh conical sieve, season with salt and pepper, and serve.

ADD THE CURRY POWDER
TO THE SOFTENED
ONIONS

ADD THE FLOUR AND
STIR IT IN

CURRIED MUSSEL SAUCE
CAN BE MADE WITH
THE JUICES FROM
OTHER SHELLFISH,
SUCH AS CLAMS

Curried Mussel Sauce

Sauce mouclade d'Aunis

This sauce accompanies to perfection mussels cooked à la marinière and taken out of their shells, or poached cod or halibut. It is also wonderful with a rice pilaff or a dish of pasta bows.

Serves 6
PREPARATION TIME: 5 MINUTES
COOKING TIME: ABOUT 25 MINUTES

Ingredients:
4 TABLESPOONS BUTTER
1/3 CUP MINCED ONION
I TABLESPOON CURRY POWDER
2 TABLESPOONS FLOUR
2 CUPS COOKING JUICES FROM MUSSELS
AND OTHER SHELLFISH, SUCH AS CLAMS
I SMALL BOUQUET GARNI (PAGE 10)
2/3 CUP HEAVY CREAM
SALT AND FRESHLY GROUND PEPPER

Melt the butter in a saucepan, add the onions, and sweat over low heat for 3 minutes. Add the curry powder and flour, stir with a wooden spoon, and cook for another 3 minutes, then pour in the cold shellfish juices. Put in the bouquet garni, bring to a boil, and leave the sauce to bubble very gently for 20 minutes, stirring with the wooden spoon every 5 minutes. Add the cream, give another bubble, then discard the bouquet garni and season the sauce with salt and pepper. Serve immediately.

ADD THE CREAM TO
THE SAUCE

REMOVE THE
BOUQUET GARNI

Bercy Sauce

Sauce Bercy

This simple, classic sauce goes well with any red- or white-fleshed fish. I enjoy it served with an unusual fish, roussette (which is a kind of shark), and also with skate.

Serves 6
PREPARATION TIME: 10 MINUTES
COOKING TIME: ABOUT 35 MINUTES

Ingredients:
4 TABLESPOONS BUTTER
1/2 CUP MINCED SHALLOTS
1 CUP DRY WHITE WINE
2/3 CUP FISH STOCK (PAGE 21)
1 3/4 CUPS FISH VELOUTÉ (PAGE 21)
JUICE OF 1/2 LEMON
2 TABLESPOONS CHOPPED PARSLEY
SALT AND FRESHLY GROUND PEPPER

Melt 1 1/2 tablespoons butter in a saucepan, add the minced shallots, and sweat them gently for 1 minute. Pour in the wine and fish stock and cook over medium heat until the liquid has reduced by half. Add the fish *velouté* and simmer gently for 20 minutes. The sauce should be thick enough to coat the back of a spoon lightly. If it is not, cook it for 5–10 minutes longer.

Remove from the heat and whisk in the remaining butter and the lemon juice. Season the sauce, stir in the chopped parsley, and serve immediately.

TARRAGON BERCY: Replace the parsley with 1 tablespoon of snipped tarragon to make a tarragon Bercy.

Parsley Nage with Lemon Grass

Nage de persil à la citronnelle

This light, fresh sauce has a gentle lemony flavor underlying the delicious aroma of parsley. Serve it with any poached or pan-fried fish, or with scallops and jumbo shrimp.

Serves 6
PREPARATION TIME: 10 MINUTES
COOKING TIME: ABOUT 30 MINUTES

Ingredients:
2 CUPS FLAT-LEAF PARSLEY, STEMS AND LEAVES
COARSELY CHOPPED
1/4 CUP CHOPPED SHALLOT
1 LEMON GRASS STALK, SPLIT LENGTHWISE
1 1/4 CUPS FISH STOCK (PAGE 21) OR
VEGETABLE STOCK (PAGE 22)
1/4 CUP HEAVY CREAM
JUICE OF 1/2 LEMON
14 TABLESPOONS BUTTER, CHILLED AND DICED
2 TABLESPOONS FINELY SNIPPED PARSLEY LEAVES
SALT AND FRESHLY GROUND PEPPER

Put the chopped parsley, shallot, lemon grass, and stock in a saucepan and cook very gently for 10 minutes. Remove the lemon grass, transfer the contents of the pan to a blender, and purée for 1 minute.

Pass the purée through a wire-mesh conical sieve into a clean saucepan, add the cream and lemon juice, and bring to a boil. Bubble until the sauce is just thick enough to coat the back of a spoon very lightly. Reduce the heat to as low as possible and incorporate the butter, a little at a time, whisking continuously. Season the sauce to taste with salt and pepper, stir in the finely snipped parsley, and serve at once.

Mandarin Sauce

Sauce à la mandarine

This sauce glows with color and warmth and is particularly good in fall or winter. Its delicious gentle flavor makes it ideal with poached white-fleshed fish. I serve it with paupiettes of sole, simply poached or filled with a lobster mousse.

Serves 4
PREPARATION TIME: 7 MINUTES
COOKING TIME: ABOUT 20 MINUTES

Ingredients:
1½ CUPS PEELED MANDARIN OR TANGERINE
SECTIONS
⅔ CUP FISH STOCK (PAGE 21)
⅔ CUP HEAVY CREAM
2 TABLESPOONS NAPOLEON MANDERINE LIQUEUR OR
GRAND MARNIER
4 TABLESPOONS BUTTER, CHILLED AND DICED
ZEST OF 1 MANDARIN OR TANGERINE, CUT IN
JULIENNE AND BLANCHED (OPTIONAL)
SALT AND FRESHLY GROUND PEPPER

Put the mandarin sections in a food processor, mix to a pulp, and rub through a fine-mesh sieve. Pour the resulting mandarin juice and the fish stock into a small saucepan, set over medium heat, and reduce by half. Add the cream and liqueur and bubble the sauce for a few minutes, until it lightly coats the back of a spoon. Pass it again through the conical sieve. Off the heat, whisk in the butter, a little at a time, to make a smooth, shiny sauce. Season to taste, then add the mandarin zest if you wish. Serve at once.

PAUPIETTES OF SOLE FILLED
WITH LOBSTER MOUSSE, SERVED
WITH MANDARIN SAUCE

POUR THE BEER OVER THE AROMATICS

REDUCE THE LIQUID BY
TWO-THIRDS; ADD THE CREAM
THEN REDUCE UNTIL THE
SAUCE IS THICK ENOUGH TO
COAT THE BACK OF A SPOON

Beer Sauce

Sauce à la bière

This sauce is excellent with braised fish steaks, like turbot or halibut. The addition of a spoonful of the braising liquid just before serving will enhance the flavor of the sauce.

Serves 4
PREPARATION TIME: 5 MINUTES
COOKING TIME: ABOUT 15 MINUTES

Ingredients:
1/2 CUP VERY FINELY SLICED SHALLOTS
1 SMALL BOUQUET GARNI (PAGE 10)
4 JUNIPER BERRIES, CRUSHED
1 1/4 CUPS MILD BEER
1 CUP HEAVY CREAM
4 TABLESPOONS BUTTER, CHILLED AND DICED
1/2 TABLESPOON FINELY SNIPPED FLAT-LEAF PARSLEY
SALT AND FRESHLY GROUND PEPPER

Put the shallots, bouquet garni, and juniper berries in a saucepan, pour in the beer, and reduce by two-thirds over medium heat. Add the cream and bubble for 5 minutes, until the sauce will lightly coat the back of a spoon. If it seems too thin, cook it for a few more minutes. Pass the sauce through a conical sieve, whisk in the butter, a small piece at a time, and finally stir in the parsley. Season to taste with salt and pepper.

WHISK IN THE BUTTER

SWIRL THE PARSLEY INTO THE BEER SAUCE

Vermouth Sauce

Sauce minute au Noilly

We used to serve this sauce with a cassolette of scallops when we first opened our restaurant Le Gavroche. It is still hugely popular with our customers, and I often serve it at The Waterside Inn with braised white fish.

Serves 4
PREPARATION TIME: 5 MINUTES
COOKING TIME: ABOUT 20 MINUTES

Ingredients:
1/3 CUP MINCED SHALLOT
1 SPRIG OF THYME
1/2 BAY LEAF
1/2 CUP NOILLY PRAT OR DRY VERMOUTH
1 1/4 CUPS FISH STOCK (PAGE 21)
2 TABLESPOONS HEAVY CREAM
A PINCH OF PAPRIKA
4 TABLESPOONS BUTTER, CHILLED AND DICED
SALT AND FRESHLY GROUND PEPPER

Put the shallot, thyme, bay leaf, and vermouth in a saucepan and reduce by one-third over high heat. Pour in the fish stock and cook over medium heat for 10 minutes, then add the cream. Reduce the sauce over high heat until it is thick enough to coat the back of a spoon. Remove the thyme and bay leaf, whisk in the paprika, and turn the heat down to low, making sure that the sauce does not boil. Whisk in the butter, a little at a time, then season with salt and pepper.

Transfer the sauce to a blender, whizz for 30 seconds until foamy, and serve immediately.

Sauternes Sauce with Pistachios

Sauce au Sauternes et aux pistaches

I like to serve this sauce with poached or steamed fillets of sole, salmon, sea bass, or turbot. Depending on the fish, I sometimes add some freshly skinned and chopped pistachios to the sauce just before serving.

ADD THE CREAM AND COOK
UNTIL THE SAUCE WILL COAT
THE BACK OF A SPOON

Serves 6
PREPARATION TIME: 10 MINUTES
COOKING TIME: ABOUT 40 MINUTES

Ingredients:
1½ TABLESPOONS BUTTER
2 CUPS THINLY SLICED BUTTON MUSHROOMS
1¼ CUPS SWEET WHITE WINE (SAUTERNES OR BARSAC)
2½ CUPS FISH STOCK (PAGE 21)
⅓ CUP BLOND ROUX (PAGE 33), COOLED
⅔ CUP HEAVY CREAM
⅓ CUP PISTACHIO BUTTER (PAGE 57)
SALT AND FRESHLY GROUND PEPPER

ADD THE MUSHROOMS
TO THE MELTED
BUTTER

Melt the butter in a saucepan, add the mushrooms, and sweat gently for 2 minutes. Pour in the wine and reduce by one-third, then add the fish stock and bring to a boil. Immediately whisk in the cooled blond roux, a little at a time. Cook the sauce at a very gentle bubble for 30 minutes, whisking it and skimming the surface every 10 minutes.

Add the cream and cook until the sauce will coat the back of a spoon, then whisk in the pistachio butter, a small piece at a time. As soon as it is all incorporated, stop the cooking, season the sauce to taste, and pass it through a fine-mesh conical sieve. Serve it within a few minutes, or keep it warm in a *bain-marie,* but do not allow it to boil.

WHISK IN THE ROUX
AND BUBBLE THE SAUCE
FOR 30 MINUTES

WHISK IN THE PISTACHIO
BUTTER

Matelote Sauce

Sauce matelote

Matelote sauce is customarily served with baby onions and tiny button mushroom caps cooked in butter. It goes very well with whole pan-fried trout, whiting, monkfish tail, and many other fish. I sometimes finish the sauce with ½ cup langoustine butter (page 57), which replaces the 4 tablespoons chilled butter. This makes it very delicate and perfect for serving with sea bass.

Serves 4
PREPARATION TIME: 5 MINUTES
COOKING TIME: ABOUT 20 MINUTES

Ingredients:
1 CUP FISH STOCK (PAGE 21)
⅔ CUP THINLY SLICED BUTTON MUSHROOMS
1¾ CUPS FISH VELOUTÉ (PAGE 21)
4 TABLESPOONS BUTTER, CHILLED AND DICED
SALT AND CAYENNE

Put the fish stock and mushrooms in a saucepan and cook over medium heat until half the liquid has evaporated. Add the fish *velouté* and bubble the sauce gently for 10 minutes, then pass it through a wire-mesh conical sieve into a clean pan. Off the heat, whisk in the butter, a little at a time. Season the sauce to taste with salt and cayenne.

RED MATELOTE SAUCE: For a red matelote, use fish stock made with red wine and substitute veal stock (page 16) for the fish *velouté* to give the sauce a deep amber color.

PAN-FRIED SEA BASS ON
SAUTERNES SAUCE WITH
PISTACHIOS

Normandy Sauce

Sauce normande

This classic sauce is wonderful not only with sole à la normande, but with any white fish. The addition of mussel juices makes it even more delicious.

Serves 6
PREPARATION TIME: 15 MINUTES
COOKING TIME: ABOUT 35 MINUTES

Ingredients:
2 TABLESPOONS BUTTER
1 1/2 CUPS THINLY SLICED BUTTON MUSHROOMS
1 SPRIG OF THYME
1/4 CUP WHITE ROUX, HOT (PAGE 33)
2 1/4 CUPS FISH STOCK, COOLED (PAGE 21)
1/4 CUP MUSSEL JUICES (OPTIONAL)
1 CUP HEAVY CREAM, MIXED WITH 3 EGG YOLKS
JUICE OF 1/2 LEMON
SALT AND FRESHLY GROUND WHITE PEPPER

In a saucepan, melt the butter over low heat, add the mushrooms and thyme, and sweat them for 2 minutes. Stir in the hot white roux, then pour in the cold fish stock and mussel juices, if you are using them. Mix with a small whisk and bring to a boil. Bubble the sauce gently for 20 minutes, stirring it with the whisk every 5 minutes. Add the cream and egg yolk mixture and the lemon juice and continue to bubble the sauce gently for 10 minutes longer. Season to taste with salt and white pepper, pass the sauce through a wire-mesh conical sieve, and serve immediately.

Seaspray Sauce

Sauce iodée

This sauce has the tang of the sea. It is excellent served with braised fish, such as turbot or halibut, or with a fish pie.

Serves 6
PREPARATION TIME: 5 MINUTES
COOKING TIME: ABOUT 25 MINUTES

Ingredients:
1 1/2 TABLESPOONS BUTTER
1/3 CUP CHOPPED SHALLOT
1 CUP FISH STOCK (PAGE 21)
2/3 CUP DRY WHITE WINE
3 TABLESPOONS MIXED DRIED AROMATICS, GROUND
OR PULVERIZED, CONSISTING OF EQUAL QUANTITIES
OF: LAVENDER FLOWERS, DILL SEEDS, LIME FLOWERS,
JUNIPER BERRIES, CORIANDER SEEDS, RED PIMENTO,
LEMON GRASS
6 SHEETS OF DRIED EDIBLE SEAWEED (NORI)
1 CUP HEAVY CREAM
6 MEDIUM OYSTERS, SHUCKED, WITH THEIR JUICES
SALT AND FRESHLY GROUND PEPPER

In a saucepan, melt the butter, add the shallot, and sweat it gently for 1 minute. Pour in the fish stock and wine, then add the mixed aromatics and seaweed and cook over medium heat until the liquid has reduced by half. Add the cream together with the oysters and their juices and bubble the sauce for 5 minutes.

Transfer the contents of the saucepan to a blender and whizz for 1 minute. Pass the sauce through a wire-mesh conical sieve into a small saucepan and stand it in a *bain-marie*. Season to taste with salt and pepper and serve immediately, or keep the sauce warm in the *bain-marie* for a few minutes.

Raspberry-Scented Oyster Sauce

Sauce aux huitres au parfum de framboises

A sauce that subtly combines the flavors of raspberries and oysters. I poach raw oysters for just 30 seconds and serve them barely warm in a little dish with this sauce and a scattering of blanched beansprouts... Quite simply sublime!

OYSTERS IN A PUFF PASTRY CASE
WITH RASPBERRY-SCENTED
OYSTER SAUCE

Serves 6
PREPARATION TIME: 5 MINUTES
COOKING TIME: ABOUT 12 MINUTES

Ingredients:
1/4 CUP CHOPPED SHALLOT
18 VERY RIPE RASPBERRIES
1 1/2 TABLESPOONS SUGAR
1/4 CUP RASPBERRY VINEGAR, HOMEMADE (PAGE 44)
OR STORE-BOUGHT
8 MEDIUM OYSTERS, SHUCKED, WITH THEIR JUICES
1 CUP HEAVY CREAM
SALT AND FRESHLY GROUND PEPPER

Combine the shallot, raspberries, and sugar in a small saucepan. Cook gently for 3–4 minutes, stirring with a wooden spoon, until you have an almost jam-like purée. Add the vinegar and bubble for 3 minutes, then add the oysters and cream, and simmer gently for 5 minutes. Pour the sauce into a blender and purée for 30 seconds, then pass it through a wire-mesh conical sieve into a clean saucepan. Season to taste and serve the sauce immediately, or keep it warm for a few minutes.

CHAPTER 7

The sauces in this chapter are refined, delicate, and unctuous, but, above all, light and airy. My favorite is hollandaise, which is glorious served warm with poached, steamed, or grilled fish, or with fresh asparagus. Numerous other sauces are derived from this wonderful, eggy emulsified creation.

Mayonnaise also forms the basis of many derivatives. It can be lightened with whipped cream, yogurt, or, if you want to reduce the calorie count, fromage blanc.

Emulsion Sauces

Also included in this chapter are whisked emulsion sauces like beurre blanc, *which should be made with a really good-quality dry white wine. This can be replaced by dry sherry if the sauce is to be served with braised white fish such as turbot.*

All these sauces are simple and quick to make. You must, however, observe a few basic rules.

* Always use a thick-bottomed stainless steel or copper saucepan with straight or sloping sides.

* Hot emulsion sauces are delicate and ethereal. They cannot be kept waiting, so must be prepared just before serving. As their cooking temperature of not more than 150°F makes them an ideal breeding ground for bacteria, they should be served immediately.

* Many emulsion sauces are prepared with raw or lightly cooked eggs. In view of health concerns over the safety of eggs, I would recommend that you use pasteurized eggs where appropriate, although if you can only find these in dried form, they are obviously not suitable for sauces such as mayonnaise. If you do use fresh eggs, make sure that they come from a reliable source, and do not serve them raw to people who may be particularly at risk, such as the elderly or very young.

* Hot emulsion sauces should not be reheated, even in a bain-marie. They will lose their lightness and may split.

* Always serve emulsion sauces in a porcelain or stainless steel sauceboat, never silver, because they will tarnish the metal and can rapidly oxidize.

CAULIFLOWER WITH
RED-PEPPER SABAYON

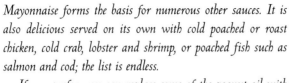

Mayonnaise

Sauce mayonnaise

Mayonnaise forms the basis for numerous other sauces. It is also delicious served on its own with cold poached or roast chicken, cold crab, lobster and shrimp, or poached fish such as salmon and cod; the list is endless.

If you prefer, you can replace some of the peanut oil with olive oil, but do not use more than one-quarter, because olive oil has a very pronounced flavor. For a creamier mayonnaise, mix in 2 tablespoons heavy cream after adding the warm vinegar or cold lemon juice.

Serves 4
PREPARATION TIME: 5 MINUTES

Ingredients:
2 EGG YOLKS
I TABLESPOON STRONG DIJON MUSTARD
I CUP PEANUT OIL
I TABLESPOON WHITE WINE VINEGAR, WARMED, OR
I TABLESPOON COLD LEMON JUICE
SALT AND FRESHLY GROUND PEPPER

ABOVE AND BELOW: WHISK
UNTIL THE MAYONNAISE
BECOMES THICK AND GLOSSY

Lay a dish towel on the work surface and stand a mixing or salad bowl on the towel. In the bowl, combine the egg yolks, mustard, and a little salt and pepper (1) and mix with a whisk (2). Pour in the oil in a thin, steady stream, whisking continuously (3). When it is all incorporated, whisk more vigorously for 30 seconds to make a thick, glossy mayonnaise, then add the hot vinegar or cold lemon juice (4). Adjust the seasoning with salt and pepper.

The mayonnaise can be kept at room temperature, covered with plastic wrap, until ready to use. However, it is not wise to keep it for more than a few hours unless you use pasteurized eggs.

MAYONNAISE MAKES A
WONDERFUL DIP FOR
CRUSTACEANS

Aïoli

L'aïoli

This sauce is excellent with salt cod, bouillabaisse (it is much better than the traditional rouille*), fish soups, and innumerable Mediterranean vegetables. Potatoes do not figure in a classic* aïoli, *but I like the rustic, creamy quality they add to the sauce.*

Serves 8
PREPARATION TIME: 15 MINUTES

Ingredients:
I CUP BAKED POTATO FLESH, RUBBED THROUGH A
SIEVE AND KEPT AT ROOM TEMPERATURE
4 GARLIC CLOVES, PEELED, GREEN SHOOT
REMOVED, AND CRUSHED (PAGE 8)
I RAW EGG YOLK
2 HARD-BOILED EGG YOLKS, RUBBED THROUGH
A SIEVE
7/8 CUP OLIVE OIL
A PINCH OF SAFFRON THREADS, INFUSED IN
3 TABLESPOONS BOILING WATER
SALT AND CAYENNE

In a mortar, combine the potato flesh, garlic, raw and cooked egg yolks, and a pinch of salt if you wish. Crush these ingredients with a pestle until well amalgamated, then start to trickle in the olive oil in a thin, steady stream, working the mixture continuously with the pestle. When about half the oil has been incorporated, add the hot saffron infusion, still mixing as you go. Trickle in the remaining oil, working it in with the pestle to make a smooth sauce. Season with a generous pinch of cayenne and salt to taste.

Rémoulade Sauce

Sauce rémoulade

This piquant sauce is perfect for a cold buffet, with assorted cold meats, or as a condiment for picnic food such as pressed tongue and roast pork or chicken.

Serves 6
PREPARATION TIME: 3 MINUTES

Ingredients:
I QUANTITY MAYONNAISE (PAGE 109)
3 TABLESPOONS MINCED CORNICHONS OR GHERKINS
2 TABLESPOONS MINCED CAPERS
I TABLESPOON SNIPPED FLAT-LEAF PARSLEY
I TABLESPOON SNIPPED CHERVIL
I TABLESPOON SNIPPED TARRAGON
I ANCHOVY FILLET, CRUSHED WITH THE FLAT OF A
CHEF'S KNIFE AND MINCED
I TEASPOON DIJON MUSTARD, CHILLED
SALT AND FRESHLY GROUND PEPPER

Put the mayonnaise in a bowl and mix in all the other ingredients with a spatula. Season to taste.

Sea-Urchin Sauce

Sauce aux oursins

Accentuate the flavor of cold crustaceans, such as lobster, crab, or shrimp, with this delicate sea-urchin sauce.

Serves 4
PREPARATION TIME: 5 MINUTES

Ingredients:
CORALS OF 12 SEA URCHINS (CUT THEM
OPEN WITH SCISSOR TIPS AND SCRAPE OUT THE
CORALS WITH A TEASPOON)
I QUANTITY MAYONNAISE (PAGE 109)
I TABLESPOON Napoleon MANDARINE LIQUEUR
OR GRAND MARNIER
1/2 CUP HEAVY CREAM, WHIPPED UNTIL THICK
6 DROPS OF HOT-PEPPER SAUCE
SALT

Rub the sea urchin corals through a fine sieve, then fold them into the mayonnaise with a whisk. Delicately fold in the other ingredients with a spatula, and season the sauce with salt.

Gribiche Sauce

Sauce gribiche

Gribiche sauce was one of those that I most often concocted during the 1960s when I was chef to Mlle. Cécile de Rothschild. She requested this sauce incessantly; she adored it served with cold fish, crustaceans, shellfish, smoked trout, and hard-boiled eggs — in fact, with almost everything.

Serves 6
PREPARATION TIME: 5 MINUTES

Ingredients:
4 FRESHLY COOKED HARD-BOILED EGG YOLKS
I TEASPOON STRONG DIJON MUSTARD
I CUP PEANUT OIL
I TABLESPOON WHITE WINE VINEGAR
WHITES OF 2 OF THE HARD-BOILED EGGS,
COARSELY CHOPPED
3 TABLESPOONS SMALL CAPERS, DRAINED, AND
CHOPPED IF THEY ARE LARGE
2 1/2 TABLESPOONS FINELY DICED CORNICHONS
2 TABLESPOONS FINES HERBES (PAGE IO), FINELY
SNIPPED
SALT AND FRESHLY GROUND PEPPER

Put the egg yolks, mustard, and a little salt and pepper in a mortar and crush with the pestle to make a smooth paste. Gradually trickle in half the oil, mixing with the pestle as you go to amalgamate it thoroughly. Still mixing, add the vinegar, then continue to trickle in the remaining oil in the same way as before. Finally, add all the other ingredients, mix them in with a spoon, and season the sauce to taste with salt and pepper.

Swedish Sauce

Sauce suédoise

This sauce makes a good accompaniment to cold roast goose or pork, or to any thinly sliced cold smoked meats.

Serves 6
PREPARATION TIME: IO MINUTES
COOKING TIME: ABOUT 20 MINUTES

Ingredients:
1/2 POUND TART-SWEET APPLES, PEELED, CORED, AND
CUT IN CHUNKS
1/4 CUP DRY WHITE WINE
I QUANTITY MAYONNAISE (PAGE IO9)
I TABLESPOON FRESHLY GRATED HORSERADISH
SALT AND FRESHLY GROUND PEPPER

Put the apples and white wine in a saucepan, cover, and cook over low heat for 15–20 minutes, until the apples are soft enough to be crushed with a fork. Remove from the heat and rub the apples through a sieve into a bowl. Reserve them in a cool place.

As soon as the apples are cold, mix them into the mayonnaise together with the horseradish, then season the sauce with salt and pepper.

Low-Calorie Mayonnaise

Sauce mayonnaise diététique

This lowfat mayonnaise can be used to accompany the same dishes as classic mayonnaise. It is refreshing and full of flavor and because it is very low in calories, it is ideal for those on a diet. If you wish, add some snipped chives, mint, tarragon, or chervil to the mayonnaise just before serving.

Serves 4
PREPARATION TIME: 3 MINUTES

Ingredients:
2/3 CUP FROMAGE BLANC
I EGG YOLK
I TEASPOON STRONG DIJON MUSTARD
I TEASPOON WHITE WINE VINEGAR OR LEMON JUICE
SALT AND FRESHLY GROUND PEPPER

Place all the ingredients in a mixing or salad bowl and whisk until completely homogeneous. Adjust the seasoning and serve.

PURÉE THE CHLOROPHYLL
INGREDIENTS (ABOVE) IN A
BLENDER

POUR THE PURÉE ONTO
THE CHEESECLOTH

FOLD UP THE EDGES OF
THE CHEESECLOTH AND
TWIST GENTLY

Green Sauce

Sauce verte

This mayonnaise-based green sauce is wonderful served with cold fish, including smoked trout and eel. The chlorophyll can be used in many other hot or cold sauces, and adds a unique herby flavor.

Serves 4
PREPARATION TIME: 40 MINUTES
COOKING TIME: ABOUT 20 MINUTES

Special equipment:
A LARGE SQUARE OF CHEESECLOTH

Ingredients:
I QUANTITY MAYONNAISE (PAGE 109)
I TABLESPOON PEANUT OIL
FINE SALT

For the chlorophyll:
2 1/2 CUPS SPINACH LEAVES, WASHED
1/4 CUP CHERVIL, WASHED AND STEMS REMOVED
2/3 CUP PARSLEY, WASHED AND STEMS REMOVED
1/3 CUP TARRAGON, WASHED AND STEMS REMOVED
1/3 CUP CHOPPED CHIVES
2 TABLESPOONS THINLY SLICED SHALLOT
2 CUPS WATER

First make the chlorophyll; you will need to do this in two batches. Put half the ingredients in a blender and whizz first at low speed for I minute, then for 4 minutes at medium speed. Scrape the resulting herb purée into a bowl; repeat with the remaining herbs.

Stretch the cheesecloth loosely over a saucepan and secure it with string to stop it slipping. Pour the herb purée into the cheesecloth and leave the liquid to filter through. When most of it has dripped into the pan, remove the string, fold up the edges of the cheesecloth, and twist gently to extract as much liquid as possible. Discard the herb purée, and rinse the cheesecloth in cold water.

Set the pan containing the bright green juice over low heat and bring to a simmer, stirring occasionally with a wooden spoon. Add a pinch of salt and, as soon as the liquid begins to tremble, remove from the heat.

POUR THE CHLOROPHYLL
ONTO THE CHEESECLOTH
AND DRAIN WELL

SCRAPE OFF THE
CHLOROPHYLL WITH A
METAL SPATULA

COVER THE CHLOROPHYLL
WITH A FILM OF OIL

ADD AS MUCH CHLOROPHYLL AS
YOU WISH TO THE MAYONNAISE

MIX THE TWO SAUCES TOGETHER
WITH A WHISK

Stretch the cheesecloth very loosely over a bowl and secure it with string as before, then delicately ladle the contents of the saucepan onto the cheesecloth. Leave for a few minutes to drain well, then use a metal spatula or spoon to scrape off the soft green purée (chlorophyll) from the surface of the cheesecloth. Place this in a small bowl, pour a trickle of peanut oil over the surface of the chlorophyll, and keep in a cool place until ready to use (it will keep in the fridge for several days).

To make the green sauce, use a whisk to stir as much of the chlorophyll as you wish into the mayonnaise. The quantity will depend on your taste and how much herb flavor you desire.

Vincent Sauce

Sauce Vincent

This sauce, which dates from the 18th century, remains very popular. It is perfect for a summer buffet and is often served with poached salmon or turbot in aspic or a chaud-froid.

Serves 6
PREPARATION TIME: 5 MINUTES

Ingredients:
$^1/_2$ QUANTITY GREEN SAUCE (OPPOSITE)
$^1/_2$ QUANTITY TARTAR SAUCE (PAGE 114)

Mix the two sauces together with a whisk.

Tartar Sauce

Sauce tartare

Tartar sauce is a classic, which is used mainly to accompany any cold cooked fish.

Serves 6
PREPARATION TIME: 5 MINUTES

Ingredients:
3 HARD-BOILED EGG YOLKS, AT ROOM TEMPERATURE
7/8 CUP PEANUT OIL
I TABLESPOON WINE VINEGAR OR LEMON JUICE
1 1/2 TABLESPOONS MINCED ONION, BLANCHED,
REFRESHED, AND WELL DRAINED
I TABLESPOON SNIPPED CHIVES
3 TABLESPOONS MAYONNAISE (PAGE 109)
SALT AND FRESHLY GROUND PEPPER

Put the egg yolks in a mortar and pound with the pestle to make a smooth paste. Season with salt and pepper, then incorporate the oil in a thin stream, stirring continuously with the pestle. When it is all incorporated, add the vinegar or lemon juice, then the onion, chives, and mayonnaise, and season to taste.

POUND THE EGG
YOLKS TO A PASTE
IN A MORTAR

ABOVE AND
RIGHT: ADD THE
OIL IN A THIN
STREAM,
STIRRING WITH
THE PESTLE
UNTIL WELL
AMALGAMATED

ADD THE ONION AND CHIVES

STIR IN THE MAYONNAISE

Alicante Sauce

Sauce Alicante

This is a cold sister sauce to Maltaise sauce (page 119), which is based on a warm hollandaise. Alicante sauce is perfect with cold asparagus, but it should not be chilled before serving. I prefer paprika to cayenne for its color and flavor, but the choice is yours. As always, once beaten egg whites have been added to the sauce, it cannot be kept waiting.

Serves 6
PREPARATION TIME: 5 MINUTES

Ingredients:
ZEST OF 1 ORANGE, MINCED, BLANCHED, REFRESHED,
AND WELL DRAINED
1 QUANTITY MAYONNAISE (PAGE 109), MADE
WITH 1 TABLESPOON LEMON JUICE AND
1 TABLESPOON ORANGE JUICE (NO VINEGAR)
2 EGG WHITES
SALT AND PAPRIKA OR CAYENNE

Whisk the orange zest into the mayonnaise and add paprika or cayenne, as you prefer. Beat the egg whites until stiff and firm them up with a pinch of salt, then delicately fold them into the mayonnaise. Serve the sauce immediately.

Bagnarotte Sauce

Sauce bagnarotte

This sauce dates back to my days as chef to Mlle. Cécile de Rothschild in Paris, and I still often serve it at The Waterside Inn, particularly with canapés in the summer. It is delicious with large shrimp or crab, ripe cherry tomatoes, or raw cauliflower florets. It must be served very cold.

Serves 6
PREPARATION TIME: 3 MINUTES

Ingredients:
1 QUANTITY MAYONNAISE (PAGE 109)
3 TABLESPOONS TOMATO KETCHUP
1 TEASPOON WORCESTERSHIRE SAUCE
1 TABLESPOON COGNAC
2 TABLESPOONS HEAVY CREAM
6 DROPS OF HOT-PEPPER SAUCE
JUICE OF $1/2$ LEMON
SALT AND FRESHLY GROUND PEPPER

Put the mayonnaise in a bowl and mix in all the other ingredients with a whisk. Season to taste with salt and pepper, and keep in the refrigerator until ready to use.

Alsatian Mustard Sauce with Horseradish

Sauce moutarde au raifort ou alsacienne

I use this sauce in winter to accompany roast or grilled fish. It is also delicious with steamed broccoli or with soft poached eggs served in a ramekin on a bed of corn sweated in butter.

Serves 6
PREPARATION TIME: 5 MINUTES
COOKING TIME: 12–15 MINUTES

Ingredients:
1 QUANTITY HOLLANDAISE SAUCE (PAGE 116)
1 TABLESPOON ENGLISH MUSTARD POWDER,
DISSOLVED IN
1 TABLESPOON COLD WATER
1 TABLESPOON GRATED HORSERADISH
SALT AND FRESHLY GROUND WHITE PEPPER

Just before serving the sauce, whisk in the lemon juice specified in the hollandaise recipe, the mustard, and horseradish. Season to taste with salt and pepper, and serve immediately.

Hollandaise Sauce

Sauce hollandaise

Hollandaise sauce is one of the great classics and many other sauces are derived from it. It is light, smooth, and delicate and does not like to be kept waiting; if you cannot serve it immediately, keep it covered in a warm place.

Serves 6 (makes about 3 cups)

PREPARATION TIME: 20 MINUTES
COOKING TIME: 12–15 MINUTES

Ingredients:
1/4 CUP COLD WATER
I TABLESPOON WHITE WINE VINEGAR
1/2 TABLESPOON WHITE PEPPERCORNS, CRUSHED
4 EGG YOLKS
I CUP BUTTER, FRESHLY CLARIFIED (PAGE 31) AND
COOLED TO TEPID
JUICE OF 1/2 LEMON
SALT

THE LEMON JUICE SHOULD BE STIRRED INTO THE HOLLANDAISE SAUCE JUST BEFORE SERVING

Combine the water, vinegar, and pepper in a small, heavy-based, stainless steel saucepan (I). Over low heat, reduce by one-third, then let cool in a cold place.

When the liquid is cold, add the egg yolks (2) and mix thoroughly with a small whisk. Set the saucepan over a very gentle heat and whisk continuously, making sure that the whisk comes into contact with the entire bottom surface of the pan (3). Keep whisking as you gently and progressively increase the heat source; the sauce should emulsify very gradually, becoming smooth and creamy after 8–10 minutes. Do not allow the temperature of the sauce to rise above 150°F.

Take the saucepan off the heat and, whisking continuously, blend in the cooled clarified butter, a little at a time (4). Season the sauce with salt to taste.

Pass the sauce through a fine-mesh conical sieve and serve as soon as possible, stirring in the lemon juice at the last moment.

NOISETTE SAUCE: 1/4 cup *beurre noisette* (browned butter) added just before serving gives hollandaise sauce a delicious flavor and transforms it into a *sauce noisette*.

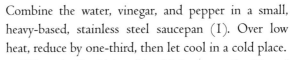

Hollandaise Sauce with Red Butter

Sauce hollandaise au beurre rouge

I like to serve this glorious sauce with grilled lobster or a piece of pan-fried cod garnished with large shrimp and braised oyster mushrooms.

Serves 6
PREPARATION TIME: 5 MINUTES
COOKING TIME: 12–15 MINUTES

Ingredients:
I QUANTITY HOLLANDAISE SAUCE (PAGE II6), MADE
WITH ONLY 2/3 CUP CLARIFIED BUTTER
I CUP LANGOUSTINE BUTTER (PAGE 57)
1/2 TABLESPOON FINELY GRATED FRESH GINGER
1/4 CUP HEAVY CREAM, WHIPPED TO A FLOPPY
CONSISTENCY WITH THE JUICE OF 1/2 LEMON
SALT AND FRESHLY GROUND PEPPER

Follow the recipe for hollandaise sauce, gradually whisking in the 2/3 cup clarified butter and the langoustine butter. Add the lemon juice specified in the hollandaise recipe and the ginger. Very gently fold in the lemony cream, season to taste with salt and pepper, and serve immediately.

Hollandaise Sauce with Fish Stock

Sauce hollandaise au fumet de poisson

This sauce is delicious with pan-fried or grilled turbot or halibut. I sometimes add a few spoons of the cooking juices from shellfish to the fish stock before reducing it, which further enhances the flavor.

Serves 6
PREPARATION TIME: 5 MINUTES
COOKING TIME: ABOUT 20 MINUTES

Ingredients:
1/2 CUP FISH STOCK (PAGE 21)
I QUANTITY HOLLANDAISE SAUCE (PAGE II6)
I TABLESPOON SNIPPED DILL
1/4 CUP HEAVY CREAM, WHIPPED TO SOFT PEAKS
SALT AND FRESHLY GROUND PEPPER

Pour the fish stock into a small saucepan and reduce over low heat to 2 tablespoons. Whisk this reduction into the hollandaise sauce, then add the lemon juice specified in the hollandaise recipe, the dill, and the cream. Season to taste and serve at once.

Mousseline Sauce

Sauce mousseline

This delicate sauce is perfect for serving with poached or steamed fish or with asparagus. When truffles are in season, I add some chopped truffle trimmings, which make the sauce even more delectable.

Serves 8
PREPARATION TIME: 5 MINUTES
COOKING TIME: 12–15 MINUTES

Ingredients:
1 QUANTITY HOLLANDAISE SAUCE (PAGE 116)
1/3 CUP HEAVY CREAM, WHIPPED TO SOFT PEAKS
SALT AND FRESHLY GROUND PEPPER

Just before serving the sauce, whisk in the lemon juice specified in the hollandaise recipe and the whipped cream. Season and serve immediately.

Maltaise Sauce

Sauce maltaise

I like to serve this with crisply cooked snow peas mixed with some orange sections and asparagus. It also goes very well with poached sea trout.

Serves 6
PREPARATION TIME: 5 MINUTES
COOKING TIME: 12–15 MINUTES

Ingredients:
JUICE OF 1 LARGE BLOOD ORANGE (PREFERABLY),
OR OF 2 SMALL ORANGES
ZEST FROM THE ORANGE, MINCED, BLANCHED,
REFRESHED, AND WELL DRAINED
1 QUANTITY HOLLANDAISE SAUCE (PAGE 116)
SALT AND FRESHLY GROUND PEPPER

Put the orange juice in a small saucepan, set over low heat, and reduce by one-third, then add the zest and take the pan off the heat. Just before serving, whisk the lemon juice specified in the hollandaise recipe into the sauce, together with the reduced orange juice. Serve immediately.

Beurre Blanc with Cream

Beurre blanc à la crème

Like all beurres blancs, *this must be made with the best-quality unsalted butter. This delicate sauce is simple to make and is delicious with almost any poached fish.*

Serves 6
PREPARATION TIME: 10 MINUTES
COOKING TIME: ABOUT 15 MINUTES

Ingredients:
1/2 CUP WHITE WINE VINEGAR
1/2 CUP MINCED SHALLOTS
2 TABLESPOONS WATER
1/4 CUP HEAVY CREAM
14 TABLESPOONS BUTTER, CHILLED AND DICED
SALT AND FRESHLY GROUND WHITE PEPPER

Combine the vinegar, shallots, and water in a small, thick-bottomed saucepan and reduce the liquid over low heat by two-thirds. Add the cream and reduce again by one-third. Over low heat, whisk in the butter, a little at a time, or beat it in with a wooden spoon. It is vital to keep the sauce barely simmering at 195°F and not to let it boil during this operation. Season with salt and pepper, and serve immediately.

BEURRE ROUGE WITH CREAM: You can make a red version of this by substituting an equal quantity of red wine vinegar for the white wine vinegar.

Cider
Beurre Blanc

Beurre blanc au cidre

I adore this butter sauce served with grilled scallops, a simply poached whole sole, or braised turbot.

Serves 6
PREPARATION TIME: 10 MINUTES
COOKING TIME: 15 MINUTES

Ingredients:
1/3 CUP CIDER VINEGAR
1/2 CUP MINCED SHALLOTS
1/2 CUP HARD CIDER
1/3 CUP PEELED AND FINELY GRATED APPLE
I CUP BUTTER, CHILLED AND DICED
SALT AND FRESHLY GROUND PEPPER

Put the vinegar and shallot in a small, thick-bottomed saucepan, set over low heat, and reduce the liquid by half. Add the cider and grated apple and cook gently to reduce the liquid by one-third. Still over low heat, incorporate the butter, a little at a time, using a whisk or small wooden spoon. The butter sauce must not boil, but merely tremble at about 195°F. Season to taste with salt and pepper and serve immediately, or keep the sauce warm for a few minutes in a *bain-marie*.

Champagne
Beurre Blanc

Beurre blanc au Champagne

This sauce is wonderful with poached chicken or guinea fowl, and equally good with whole braised fish, such as John Dory, sole, or baby turbot.

Serves 6
PREPARATION TIME: 10 MINUTES
COOKING TIME: ABOUT 20 MINUTES

Ingredients:
1/4 CUP CHAMPAGNE VINEGAR
1/2 CUP MINCED SHALLOTS
I SPRIG OF THYME
1/2 CUP BRUT CHAMPAGNE
3/4 CUP VERY FINELY DICED BUTTON MUSHROOMS
I CUP BUTTER, CHILLED AND DICED
SALT AND FRESHLY GROUND WHITE PEPPER

Combine the vinegar, shallots, and thyme in a small, thick-bottomed saucepan and reduce the liquid by half over low heat. Add the champagne and mushrooms and continue to cook gently until the liquid has again reduced by half. Remove the thyme. Over low heat, whisk in the butter, a little at a time, or beat it in with a wooden spoon. It is vital to keep the sauce barely simmering at 195°F and not to let it boil during this operation. Season to taste and serve the sauce at once, or keep it hot in a *bain-marie* for a few minutes.

CIDER BEURRE BLANC
WITH SCALLOPS

ADD THE CHOPPED BELL
PEPPER TO THE SAUCEPAN

SIMMER FOR 15 MINUTES,
THEN WHISK THE EGG YOLKS
INTO THE ALMOST COLD
SAUCE

Red~Pepper Sabayon

Sabayon au poivron rouge

I serve this sabayon with poached eggs on a bed of pilaff rice, or with vegetables like cauliflower and asparagus. It is also good with grilled fish, particularly salmon.

The vegetable stock can be replaced by chicken or fish stock, depending on the dish the sauce is to accompany.

Serves 4
PREPARATION TIME: 10 MINUTES
COOKING TIME: ABOUT 25 MINUTES

Ingredients:
1/2 POUND RED BELL PEPPERS
1 CUP VEGETABLE STOCK (PAGE 22)
1 SMALL SPRIG OF THYME
4 EGG YOLKS
4 TABLESPOONS BUTTER, CHILLED AND DICED
SALT AND FRESHLY GROUND PEPPER

Halve the red peppers lengthwise and remove the stems, seeds, and white membranes. Coarsely chop the peppers, place in a small saucepan with the stock and thyme, and simmer for 15 minutes. Pour the contents of the saucepan into a blender and whizz for 1 minute. Pass the purée through a wire-mesh conical sieve into a small clean saucepan and leave until almost cold, then whisk in the egg yolks. Stand the pan in a *bain-marie* or over indirect heat and whisk the *sabayon* to a ribbon consistency. Whisk in the butter, a little at a time, season the *sabayon* with salt and pepper, and serve at once.

RIGHT: HALVE THE
PEPPERS LENGTHWISE

WHISK TO A RIBBON
CONSISTENCY

WHISK THE BUTTER INTO
THE SAUCE

Béarnaise Sauce

Sauce béarnaise

This sauce is wonderful with grilled steak and beef fondue. I eat it just on its own, spread on a piece of bread.

Serves 6
PREPARATION TIME: 20 MINUTES
COOKING TIME: 12–15 MINUTES

Ingredients:
2 TABLESPOONS WHITE WINE VINEGAR
3 TABLESPOONS SNIPPED TARRAGON
1/4 CUP MINCED SHALLOT
10 PEPPERCORNS, CRUSHED
4 EGG YOLKS
3 TABLESPOONS COLD WATER
I CUP FRESHLY CLARIFIED BUTTER (PAGE 31),
COOLED TO TEPID
2 TABLESPOONS SNIPPED CHERVIL
JUICE OF 1/2 LEMON
SALT AND FRESHLY GROUND PEPPER

Combine the vinegar, 2 tablespoons tarragon, the shallot, and peppercorns in a small, thick-bottomed saucepan, and reduce by half over low heat. Set aside in a cool place.

When the vinegar reduction is cold, add the egg yolks and cold water. Set the pan over low heat and whisk continuously, making sure that the whisk reaches right down into the bottom of the pan. As you whisk, gently increase the heat; the sauce should emulsify slowly and gradually, becoming unctuous after 8–10 minutes. Do not let it become hotter than 150°F.

Remove from the heat and whisk the clarified butter into the sauce, a little at a time. Season with salt and pepper and pass the sauce through a wire-mesh conical sieve into another pan. Stir in the rest of the tarragon, the chervil, and lemon juice, and serve at once.

CHORON SAUCE: 2 tablespoons well-reduced cooked tomato coulis (page 66) added to the béarnaise will give you a Choron sauce.

FOYOT SAUCE: Add 2 tablespoons veal *demi-glace* (page 16) to the béarnaise to make a Foyot sauce.

Paloise Sauce

Sauce paloise

This is basically a béarnaise sauce flavored with mint instead of tarragon. It is excellent with roast or grilled lamb, and often appears on the menu at The Waterside Inn.

Serves 6
PREPARATION TIME: 20 MINUTES
COOKING TIME: 12–15 MINUTES

Ingredients:
I QUANTITY BÉARNAISE SAUCE (LEFT), MADE
WITHOUT TARRAGON
I TABLESPOON SNIPPED MINT LEAVES

Follow the recipe for béarnaise sauce, substituting two-thirds of the mint for the tarragon. Pass the sauce through a wire-mesh conical sieve, then add the lemon juice, chervil, and the remaining mint. Serve immediately.

GRILLED LAMB CHOPS
WITH PALOISE SAUCE

CHAPTER 8

The ivory paleness, creamy whiteness, or delicate blond coloring of these sauces makes them appealing and easy on the eye. Their main components are white chicken or lamb stock (made without coloring the bones or carcasses), or milk, often with the addition of some cream.

White Sauces

They are usually thickened with a white or blond roux or egg yolks, or they may be bound or smoothed with butter. Herbs, spices, relishes, white wine, or sherry add an extra dimension and individuality.

The best way to eat these light, adaptable sauces is with a spoon. They are at their most appealing in the winter, served with poached or boiled poultry, white meats, variety meats, and certain fish.

The king of the white sauces is béchamel, from which many other sauces derive, each as delicious as the last. Through the centuries, béchamel has continued to top the hit parade of our culinary heritage.

MACARONI AU GRATIN MADE
WITH A BÉCHAMEL SAUCE

Béchamel Sauce

Sauce béchamel

This is the ideal sauce for any number of dishes, such as cauliflower or endive au gratin, *macaroni and cheese made with a touch of cream and grated Gruyère or Emmenthal, a* genuine *croque monsieur — the list is endless. Like hollandaise, mayonnaise, and crème anglaise, béchamel forms the basis of innumerable other sauces.*

Serves 4
PREPARATION TIME: 5 MINUTES
COOKING TIME: ABOUT 25 MINUTES

Ingredients:
^{1}/4 CUP WHITE ROUX (PAGE 33), COOLED
2^1/2 CUPS MILK
FRESHLY GRATED NUTMEG (OPTIONAL)
SALT AND FRESHLY GROUND WHITE PEPPER

STIR THE BÉCHAMEL
CONTINUOUSLY WHILE
COOKING

SEASON WITH A LITTLE
NUTMEG (OPTIONAL)

Put the cold roux into a small, thick-bottomed saucepan. Bring the milk to a boil and pour it onto the roux, mixing and stirring with a whisk or wooden spatula. Set the pan over low heat and bring the mixture to a boil, still stirring continuously. As soon as it reaches boiling point, reduce the heat and cook at a very gentle simmer for about 20 minutes, stirring the sauce continuously and making sure that the whisk scrapes across all the surfaces of the pan.

Season the sauce with salt, white pepper, and a very little nutmeg if you wish, then pass it through a conical strainer. You can serve it immediately or keep it warm in a *bain-marie*, in which case dot a few flakes of butter over the surface to prevent a skin from forming.

Béchamel sauce will keep in an airtight container in the refrigerator for a maximum of 4 days.

CLASSIC RICH BÉCHAMEL: The old classic rich béchamel was made with the addition of veal. To make this, sweat ^{1}/2 cup diced veal and ^{1}/4 cup chopped onion in 2 tablespoons butter (1). In another pan make a basic béchamel (2 and 3); when it reaches boiling point, add the veal and onions (4) and continue with the recipe as above.

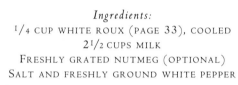

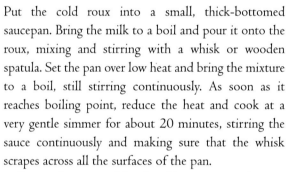

PASS THE BÉCHAMEL SAUCE
THROUGH A CONICAL
STRAINER

DOT FLAKES OF BUTTER
OVER THE SURFACE TO
PREVENT A SKIN FROM
FORMING

1 2 3 4

Coconut and Chili Sauce

Sauce à la noix de coco et aux piments

Serve this unusual, spicy sauce with wide noodles or any poached firm-fleshed white fish.

Serves 8
PREPARATION TIME: 10 MINUTES
COOKING TIME: 25 MINUTES

Ingredients:
7 TABLESPOONS BUTTER
1 SMALL HOT RED CHILI, SEEDED AND MINCED
2 JALAPEÑO PEPPERS, SEEDED AND MINCED
1/2 POUND SMALL PEELED COOKED SHRIMP
(OPTIONAL)

For the coconut béchamel:
2 1/2 TABLESPOONS BUTTER
3 TABLESPOONS FLOUR
2 CUPS CANNED COCONUT MILK
FRESHLY GRATED NUTMEG
SALT AND FRESHLY GROUND PEPPER
1 TABLESPOON SOY SAUCE
2 GARLIC CLOVES, CRUSHED OR MINCED

ADD THE CHOPPED CHILIES TO THE BROWNED BUTTER

First make the coconut béchamel. In a small saucepan, melt the butter and stir in the flour to make a roux. Cook over low heat for 2 minutes, stirring all the time with a whisk. Add the coconut milk and bring to a boil, then immediately season with nutmeg, salt, and pepper. Cook gently for 20 minutes, stirring continuously. Remove from the heat and stir in the soy sauce and garlic.

In another small saucepan, heat the 7 tablespoons butter until it turns fragrant and golden brown. Toss in the chili peppers and immediately tip the mixture into the coconut béchamel; stir until well amalgamated. Adjust the seasoning if necessary and stir in the shrimp at the last moment, if you are using them. Serve the sauce hot.

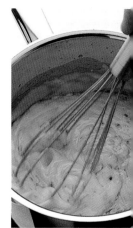

ADD THE MIXTURE TO THE COCONUT BÉCHAMEL

STIR UNTIL WELL AMALGAMATED, THEN ADD THE SHRIMP (OPTIONAL)

Aurora Sauce

Sauce Aurore

Hard-boiled eggs sliced into disks, coated with Aurora sauce, and browned under the broiler are delicious. The sauce is also very good with poached eggs, pasta, cauliflower, or broiled turkey scallops.

You can substitute a chicken velouté *(page 132) for the béchamel if you prefer the flavor.*

The taste of tomato coulis will vary according to the season; if it is highly scented and colored, use a little less. If it is pallid and lacking in intensity, use more.

Serves 6
PREPARATION TIME: 5 MINUTES
COOKING TIME: ABOUT 15 MINUTES

Ingredients:
1 1/4 CUPS BÉCHAMEL SAUCE (PAGE 128)
1/2 CUP HEAVY CREAM
1/2 CUP COOKED TOMATO COULIS (PAGE 66)
1 1/2 TABLESPOONS BUTTER, CHILLED AND DICED
SALT AND FRESHLY GROUND PEPPER OR NUTMEG

Combine the béchamel and cream in a saucepan and bring to a boil over low heat, stirring continuously with a whisk. Bubble the sauce for 5 minutes, then add the tomato coulis. Bring the sauce back to a boil and cook for 5 minutes longer, whisking continuously. Remove from the heat and whisk in the butter, a little at a time. Season the sauce with salt and pepper or nutmeg, according to taste, pass it through a wire-mesh conical sieve, and serve immediately.

Bread Sauce

The perfect sauce to accompany roast chicken or turkey. It is also ideal with roast pheasant or grouse. I often serve it at the restaurant and frequently request it at home.

Serves 4
PREPARATION TIME: 5 MINUTES
COOKING TIME: ABOUT 1 HOUR

Ingredients:
1 1/2 TABLESPOONS BUTTER
1/3 CUP CHOPPED ONIONS
1 3/4 CUPS MILK
1 SMALL ONION STUDDED WITH 2 CLOVES
3 CUPS WHITE BREAD, CRUSTS REMOVED, CUT IN CUBES
1/4 CUP HEAVY CREAM
SALT AND FRESHLY GROUND WHITE PEPPER

Melt the butter in a small saucepan, add the chopped onions, and sweat them gently for 1 minute. Pour in the milk, add the clove-studded onion, and simmer at about 195°F for 20 minutes. Stir in the bread and bring to a boil. Lower the heat and cook the sauce gently for 30 minutes, stirring occasionally with a wooden spoon. Remove the studded onion, add the cream, and bubble the sauce gently for 5 minutes, whisking gently. Season with salt and white pepper, and serve hot.

Albufera Sauce

Sauce Albufera

This is a sauce for a grand dinner. Poultry, sweetbreads, or poached veal tongue will all benefit from its richness.

Serves 6
PREPARATION TIME: 5 MINUTES

Ingredients:
2 CUPS BOILING CHICKEN VELOUTÉ (PAGE 132)
2/3 CUP VEAL *DEMI-GLACE* (PAGE 16)
1/4 CUP FRESH OR PRESERVED TRUFFLE JUICE (OPTIONAL)
SALT AND CAYENNE

Into the boiling chicken *velouté*, whisk the veal *demi-glace* and truffle juice, if using. Season the sauce with salt and cayenne to taste, and serve immediately.

Chicken Velouté

Velouté de volaille

This velouté *can be used as a base for other sauces; just omit the sherry. Personally, I find it excellent just as it is. I serve it with poached poultry and rice or with a whole pan-fried veal sweetbread garnished with leaf spinach.*

Serves 6 (makes about 3 1/2 cups)
PREPARATION TIME: 5 MINUTES
COOKING TIME: ABOUT 30 MINUTES

Ingredients:
1/4 CUP WHITE ROUX, HOT (PAGE 33)
3 CUPS CHICKEN STOCK, COOLED (PAGE 18)
1/4 CUP DRY SHERRY (OPTIONAL)
SALT AND FRESHLY GROUND WHITE PEPPER

Put the hot white roux into a saucepan and add the cold chicken stock. Set over medium heat and bring to a boil, whisking continuously. Reduce the heat and gently simmer the *velouté* for 30 minutes, stirring the sauce and skimming the surface every 10 minutes. Add the sherry if you are using it, and cook for 1 more minute. Season the sauce with salt and white pepper, and pass it through a wire-mesh conical sieve.

Sauce Albert

Sauce Albert, which we serve with our pot-au-feu, *and cuts like veal shanks and beef flank, is one of the legendary Roux brothers' sauces, which our faithful regulars always enjoy. It is also excellent with roast rabbit.*

Serves 4
PREPARATION TIME: 15 MINUTES
COOKING TIME: ABOUT 50 MINUTES

Ingredients:
1 1/4 CUPS CHICKEN STOCK (PAGE 18),
OR BROTH FROM A POT-AU-FEU
2/3 CUP FRESHLY GRATED HORSERADISH, OR 1 CUP
DRAINED BOTTLED HORSERADISH
1 1/4 CUPS HEAVY CREAM
1 2/3 CUPS FRESH WHITE BREAD, CRUSTS REMOVED,
CUT IN SMALL CUBES
1 EGG YOLK
1 TEASPOON ENGLISH MUSTARD POWDER,
DISSOLVED IN 1 TABLESPOON COLD WATER
SALT AND FRESHLY GROUND WHITE PEPPER

Combine the chicken stock or broth and the horseradish in a small saucepan, set over medium heat, and boil for 15 minutes. Add the cream and bubble gently for 20 minutes longer. Transfer the sauce to a blender and whizz for 1 minute (you may have to do this in two batches), then pass the sauce through a wire-mesh conical sieve into a clean saucepan.

Add the cubes of bread and cook the sauce over low heat for 10 minutes, whisking continuously. Remove from the heat, add the egg yolk and mustard, and stir for a few moments before vigorously whisking the sauce to make it very smooth; it should have the consistency of oatmeal. Season to taste with salt and pepper, and serve at once. If you need to keep the sauce warm, do not let it boil.

Mustard and White-Wine Sauce

Sauce moutarde au vin blanc

This versatile sauce is perfect served with pot-roasted poultry or white meats. For these, make the sauce with chicken stock, but obviously if you are going to serve it with poached or braised fish (preferably firm-fleshed), use fish stock instead.

Serves 4
PREPARATION TIME: 10 MINUTES
COOKING TIME: ABOUT 40 MINUTES

Ingredients:
2 TABLESPOONS BUTTER
I CUP THINLY SLICED BUTTON MUSHROOMS
1/2 CUP MINCED SHALLOTS
A PINCH OF CURRY POWDER
I TABLESPOON COGNAC OR ARMAGNAC
I CUP DRY WHITE WINE
I SMALL BOUQUET GARNI (PAGE 10)
I CUP FISH STOCK (PAGE 21)
OR CHICKEN STOCK (PAGE 18)
1 1/4 CUPS HEAVY CREAM
I TEASPOON ENGLISH MUSTARD POWDER, DISSOLVED
IN A LITTLE WATER
2 TABLESPOONS WHOLEGRAIN MUSTARD
SALT AND FRESHLY GROUND PEPPER

SWEAT THE
MUSHROOMS IN
THE BUTTER

ADD THE COGNAC
AND THE WINE

In a saucepan, melt the butter, add the mushrooms and shallot, and sweat for I minute. Stir in the curry powder and add the cognac and wine. Bring to a boil, put in the bouquet garni, and reduce the liquid by one-third. Pour in the fish or chicken stock, and bubble for 5 minutes, then add the cream and the English mustard, and cook until the sauce is thick enough to coat the back of a spoon. Remove the bouquet garni, season to taste with salt and pepper, and pass the sauce through a wire-mesh conical strainer. Stir in the wholegrain mustard. The sauce is now ready to serve.

COOK UNTIL THE SAUCE WILL
COAT THE BACK OF THE SPOON

STIR IN THE WHOLEGRAIN
MUSTARD

Parsley Sauce

Sauce au persil

This sauce is simplicity itself and most delicious, especially when it is prepared with the cooking liquid from a boiled ham and served with the ham. It also tastes good with plain boiled Brussels sprouts, carrots, or potatoes.

You can enrich the sauce with cream or butter, but I prefer it without. Because it is not rich, it can be eaten with a spoon; this is why I suggest that the recipe serves four people rather than six, as you might expect.

Serves 4
PREPARATION TIME: 5 MINUTES
COOKING TIME: ABOUT 20 MINUTES

Ingredients:
1 1/2 CUPS COOKING LIQUID FROM A BOILED HAM,
OR CHICKEN STOCK (PAGE 18)
2/3 CUP MILK
3 TABLESPOONS WHITE ROUX, COOLED (PAGE 33)
2 TABLESPOONS CHOPPED PARSLEY
A PINCH OF FRESHLY GRATED NUTMEG
SALT AND FRESHLY GROUND WHITE PEPPER

Bring the cooking liquid or stock and the milk to a boil. Put the cold roux in a saucepan and pour on the hot liquid, whisking as you go. Bring to a boil over low heat, stirring continuously with the whisk as the sauce begins to bubble. Add the parsley and simmer the sauce for 15 minutes, skimming the surface with a spoon if necessary. Season with the nutmeg and salt and pepper to taste, and serve piping hot.

Supreme Sauce with Sherry

Sauce suprême au sherry

A classic supreme sauce is made without sherry, but I think it adds a theatrical note which pleases me very much. This wonderfully smooth, creamy sauce is subtle and savory. Serve it with poached poultry, timbales of mushrooms and sweetbreads, braised lettuce, or thin pan-fried veal cutlets. It is essential to use the best-quality butter to finish this sauce.

Serves 4
PREPARATION TIME: 5 MINUTES
COOKING TIME: ABOUT 10 MINUTES

Ingredients:
1 CUP BOILING CHICKEN VELOUTÉ (PAGE 132)
2/3 CUP THINLY SLICED BUTTON MUSHROOMS
1/4 CUP HEAVY CREAM
2 TABLESPOONS BUTTER, CHILLED AND DICED
1/4 CUP DRY SHERRY
SALT AND FRESHLY GROUND PEPPER

Pour the boiling chicken *velouté* into a saucepan and add the mushrooms and cream. Simmer over low heat for 10 minutes, stirring occasionally with a wooden spoon. Pass the sauce through a wire-mesh conical sieve into a clean saucepan, turn the heat to low, and whisk in the butter, a little at a time. Remove from the heat, stir in the sherry, season the sauce with salt and pepper, and serve immediately.

BOILED HAM WITH PARSLEY SAUCE

Caper Sauce with Anchovies

Sauce aux câpres au parfum d'anchois

A lively, vigorous sauce that will cut the richness of variety meats such as brains, sweetbreads, tripe, or calf's head.

Serves 8
PREPARATION TIME: 5 MINUTES
COOKING TIME: 15 MINUTES

Ingredients:
2 CUPS CHICKEN VELOUTÉ (PAGE 132)
1 BOUQUET GARNI (PAGE 10), INCLUDING
2 SPRIGS OF SAVORY
1/2 CUP DRY WHITE WINE
1/2 CUP HEAVY CREAM
1/4 CUP ANCHOVY BUTTER (PAGE 57)
2 1/2 TABLESPOONS SMALL CAPERS (CHOP THEM IF THEY ARE LARGE), WELL DRAINED
2 ANCHOVY FILLETS, FINELY DICED
SALT AND CAYENNE

In a saucepan, bring the *velouté* to a boil, add the bouquet garni and white wine, and cook gently for 10 minutes. Pour in the cream and continue to cook gently for 5 minutes longer. The sauce should lightly coat the back of a spoon; if it is not thick enough, increase the heat to as high as possible and reduce it for a few more minutes. Lower the heat to minimum and whisk in the anchovy butter, a little at a time. Pass the sauce through a wire-mesh conical sieve into a clean saucepan. Season with cayenne and a very little salt, stir in the capers and diced anchovies, and serve at once.

Champagne Sauce with Morels

Sauce Champagne aux morilles

This is the champagne sauce that I serve with poached capon. Try this unctuous sauce for a special occasion.

Serves 8
PREPARATION TIME: 10 MINUTES
COOKING TIME: 45 MINUTES

Ingredients:
3 OUNCES FRESH MORELS, OR 1 OUNCE DRIED MORELS REHYDRATED IN BOILING WATER FOR 1 HOUR
1 3/4 CUPS CHICKEN VELOUTÉ (PAGE 132)
1 CUP BRUT CHAMPAGNE
1 CUP HEAVY CREAM
1/3 CUP FOIE-GRAS BUTTER (PAGE 63)
SALT AND FRESHLY GROUND WHITE PEPPER

First clean the fresh morels. Trim the very bottom of the stems, halve the mushrooms (or quarter them if they are very large), rinse in cold water to remove all traces of grit, and delicately pat dry on a dish towel. If you are using dried morels, drain them from their soaking water and proceed as for fresh morels.

Combine the chicken *velouté* and three-quarters of the champagne in a saucepan and boil over medium heat for 20 minutes. Put the cream and prepared morels in another saucepan and bring to a boil over medium heat. Cook for 5 minutes, then tip the cream and morel mixture into the pan with the *velouté*. Cook at a bare simmer for 15 minutes, removing any skin from the surface with a spoon if necessary.

Add the remaining champagne, bubble the sauce for 2 minutes, and remove from the heat. Add the foie-gras butter, a little at a time, mixing it into the sauce with a wooden spoon. Season with salt and white pepper, and serve immediately.

RABBIT WITH SORREL SAUCE

Sorrel Sauce

Sauce à l'oseille

This sauce is one of my mother's favorites. Its hint of acidity and freshness makes it ideal for serving with pan-fried lamb chops or roast saddle of rabbit. A few shredded mint leaves added to the sauce just before serving intensify the taste of the sorrel and make the sauce more rounded.

Serves 6
PREPARATION TIME: 5 MINUTES
COOKING TIME: ABOUT 20 MINUTES

Ingredients:
2 OUNCES SORREL
2 TABLESPOONS BUTTER
$^1/_3$ CUP MINCED SHALLOT
$^1/_2$ CUP WHITE WINE
I CUP VEGETABLE STOCK (PAGE 22)
I CUP HEAVY CREAM
SALT AND FRESHLY GROUND PEPPER

Wash the sorrel and remove the stems. Pile up several leaves, roll them up like a cigar, and shred them finely, repeating until you have shredded all the sorrel. Melt the butter in a deep frying pan, add the shallot, and sweat it over low heat for 30 seconds, then put in the sorrel and sweat gently for I more minute. Pour in the wine and stock and reduce the liquid by two-thirds. Add the cream and bubble for 2 minutes. The sauce should be thick enough to coat the back of a spoon lightly. Season to taste, and serve immediately.

Soubise Sauce

Sauce soubise

Perfect for winter, this sauce goes particularly well with roast rack or loin of veal and with roast chicken or guinea fowl. It can be prepared in advance and reheated in a bain-marie.

Serves 4
PREPARATION TIME: 5 MINUTES
COOKING TIME: 25 MINUTES

Ingredients:
3 TABLESPOONS BUTTER
1 1/2 CUPS THINLY SLICED ONIONS
1 QUANTITY BÉCHAMEL SAUCE (PAGE 128)
2/3 CUP HEAVY CREAM
FRESHLY GRATED NUTMEG
SALT AND FRESHLY GROUND PEPPER

In a saucepan, melt the butter over low heat, add the onions, and sweat for 5 minutes without coloring, stirring gently with a wooden spoon. Add the béchamel, bring to a boil over low heat, and bubble gently for 10 minutes, still stirring delicately with the wooden spoon.

Pass the sauce through a wire-mesh sieve into a clean saucepan, pressing the onions through with a wooden pounder or the back of a small ladle. Add the cream and cook gently for 6–8 minutes, stirring continuously, until the sauce thickens to the consistency of oatmeal. Season to taste with nutmeg, salt, and pepper, and serve piping hot.

Butter Sauce

Sauce bâtarde

This water-based sauce (literally "bastard sauce" in French) relies for all its flavor on the liaison mixture and the butter, which must be of excellent quality. Serve it with poached fish and asparagus, or with boiled vegetables when you want to enhance their flavor without drowning it.

Serves 8
PREPARATION TIME: 10 MINUTES
COOKING TIME: ABOUT 2 MINUTES

Ingredients:
1/4 CUP WHITE ROUX, COOLED (PAGE 33)
2 1/2 CUPS BOILING WATER
1/2 CUP BUTTER, CHILLED AND DICED
SALT AND A PINCH OF CAYENNE

For the liaison:
3 EGG YOLKS MIXED WITH THE JUICE OF
1/2 LEMON AND 2 TABLESPOONS HEAVY CREAM

Put the cold white roux in a saucepan, pour on the boiling water, and whisk thoroughly. Set over high heat and bring to a boil, whisking continuously. Boil for 2 or 3 minutes, then remove from the heat and whisk in the liaison mixture. Pass the sauce through a wire-mesh conical sieve into a clean saucepan and whisk in the chilled butter, a little at a time. Season the sauce with salt and cayenne, and serve at once.

Mornay Sauce

Sauce Mornay

You can coat a multitude of dishes with this sauce and immediately brown them lightly under a hot broiler or salamander; poached eggs, fish, vegetables, and white meats are all excellent served this way. Mixed with macaroni, mornay sauce also makes a delicious macaroni and cheese.

Serves 4
PREPARATION TIME: 5 MINUTES
COOKING TIME: ABOUT 2 MINUTES

Ingredients:
1 QUANTITY BOILING BÉCHAMEL SAUCE (PAGE 128)
1/4 CUP HEAVY CREAM MIXED WITH 3 EGG YOLKS
1 CUP GRATED EMMENTHAL, GRUYÈRE, OR
FARMHOUSE CHEDDAR
SALT AND FRESHLY GROUND PEPPER

Add the cream and egg yolk mixture to the boiling béchamel and bubble for 1 minute, whisking vigorously. Remove from the heat and mix in your chosen cheese with a wooden spoon. Season the sauce with salt and pepper, and use it as you wish.

White Bordelaise or Bonnefoy Sauce

Sauce bordelaise blanche ou Bonnefoy

This robust, well-structured sauce makes the perfect accompaniment to fish with a rather bland flavor, such as whiting, lemon sole, or farmed trout.

Serves 4
PREPARATION TIME: 5 MINUTES
COOKING TIME: ABOUT 30 MINUTES

Ingredients:
1 1/4 CUPS DRY WHITE WINE
2 TABLESPOONS COGNAC
1/2 CUP MINCED SHALLOTS
1 BOUQUET GARNI (PAGE 10)
1 3/4 CUPS FISH VELOUTÉ (PAGE 21)
3 TABLESPOONS BUTTER, CHILLED AND DICED
1 TABLESPOON SNIPPED TARRAGON LEAVES
SALT AND FRESHLY GROUND PEPPER

Combine the wine, cognac, shallots, and bouquet garni in a saucepan and reduce the liquid to one-third over high heat. Add the fish *velouté* and bubble the sauce gently for 20 minutes, skimming the surface whenever necessary. Pass the sauce through a wire-mesh conical sieve into a clean pan, then whisk in the butter, a little at a time. Season the sauce with salt and pepper, stir in the tarragon, and serve at once.

Allemande Sauce

Sauce allemande

This light, silky sauce goes very well with poached poultry, brains, and sweetbreads.

Serves 6
PREPARATION TIME: 5 MINUTES
COOKING TIME: 35 MINUTES

Ingredients:
1/2 CUP MINCED SHALLOTS
1/2 CUP DRY WHITE WINE
10 WHITE PEPPERCORNS, CRUSHED
1 BOUQUET GARNI (PAGE 10),
INCLUDING A SPRIG OF SAVORY
2 CUPS CHICKEN STOCK (PAGE 18)
1 1/3 CUPS SLICED BUTTON MUSHROOMS
1 CUP HEAVY CREAM
SALT AND FRESHLY GROUND WHITE PEPPER

For the liaison:
1/2 CUP HEAVY CREAM, WHIPPED TO
SOFT PEAKS, MIXED WITH 3 EGG YOLKS
AND THE JUICE OF 1 LEMON

Combine the shallots, white wine, crushed peppercorns, and bouquet garni in a saucepan, set over medium heat, and reduce the wine by two-thirds. Add the chicken stock and mushrooms and cook until the liquid has reduced by half. Pour in the cream and bubble the sauce for 5 minutes, or until it lightly coats the back of a spoon.

Pour in the liaison mixture, whisking to amalgamate it thoroughly. Immediately remove from the heat, season the sauce with salt and white pepper, pass it through a wire-mesh conical sieve, and serve at once.

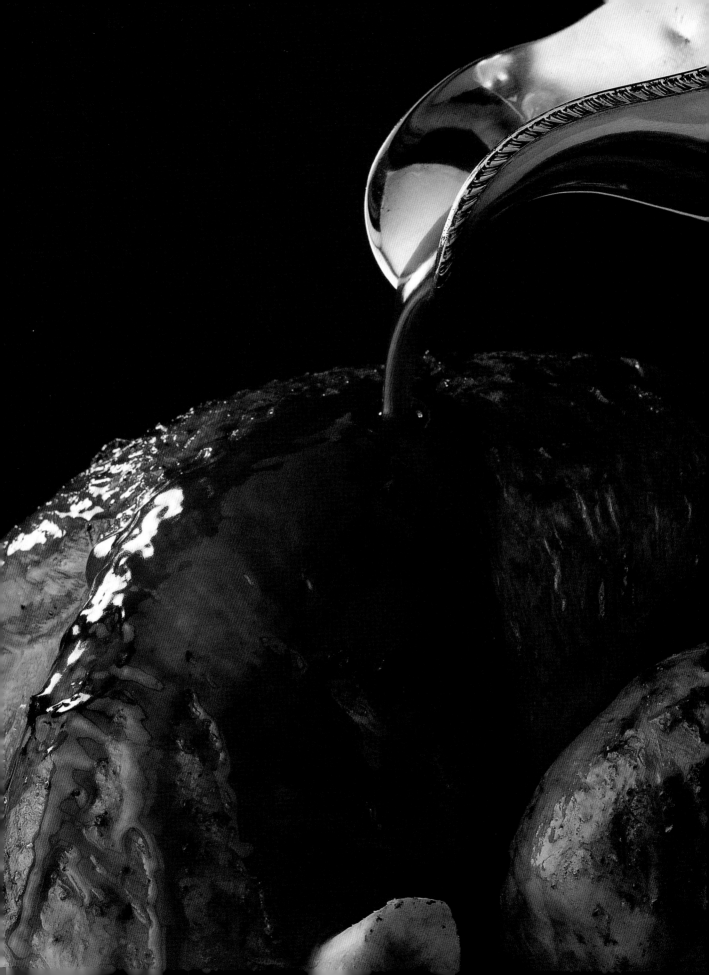

CHAPTER 9

Until the 1960s, the most frequently used and best known brown sauce was espagnole, the ultimate classic sauce that had exemplified French cuisine for generations. It reigned supreme in the kitchens of palaces, hotels, and starred restaurants, where it was used as a base or an essential element in any number of sauces, often making them over-rich and heavy.

Brown Sauces

Nowadays, it is really not practical to make this sauce, which is extremely expensive in terms of both ingredients and time: it takes twenty hours or so to complete the two cooking stages — first a brown stock, then the espagnole itself.

I shall always remember the early days of my career, when I was apprenticed to the sauce chef and had to perform the most humble of tasks — the ritual hourly skimming of the stock to ensure that the finished sauce was crystal-clear, with no impurities to impair the flavor. I can see my adolescent face reflected on the surface of the huge stockpot, blurred at first, but becoming clearer and clearer over the hours...

For the past thirty years, veal stock has replaced espagnole sauce in my kitchen. I make it without any thickening agents, so that it is, in fact, a blond veal sauce. It forms the basis of many of my brown sauces, making them velvety, delicate, and well-balanced, without masking their vital individuality. When appropriate, I substitute lamb, chicken, or duck stock to enhance the flavor of the dish they will accompany.

Brown sauces are among my favorites. They are generally robust, rich, and elegant, with a flavor that lingers on the palate. I love their warm, shimmering colors, which range from pale golden to a deep purplish-brown.

ROAST TURKEY
WITH BUCCANEER'S SAUCE

Buccaneer's Sauce

Sauce boucanière

I serve this sauce with veal chops at The Waterside Inn and garnish them with slices of banana pan-fried in butter. You can serve poultry in the same way; the sauce and garnish go well with roast chicken and turkey as well as with roast veal.

Serves 8
PREPARATION TIME: 5 MINUTES
COOKING TIME: ABOUT 25 MINUTES

Ingredients:
1 BANANA
7 TABLESPOONS BUTTER
1/2 CUP MINCED SHALLOTS OR ONIONS
3 TABLESPOONS MINCED FRESH GINGER
6 TABLESPOONS RASPBERRY VINEGAR, HOMEMADE
(PAGE 44) OR STORE-BOUGHT
1 3/4 CUPS VEAL STOCK (PAGE 16)
SALT AND FRESHLY GROUND BLACK PEPPER

Peel the banana and cut it in rounds.

Melt half the butter in a saucepan, add the minced shallots or onions, and sweat for 1 minute over medium heat. Add the ginger and cook until very lightly colored, stirring continuously with a spatula. Still stirring, add the banana slices and cook over low heat for 2 minutes, until the banana softens and begins to disintegrate. Immediately add the raspberry vinegar and continue to cook over very low heat for another 2 minutes, still stirring.

Add the veal stock and simmer the sauce gently for 20 minutes, then pass it through a conical strainer into another pan. Whisk in the remaining butter, a little at a time, until the sauce is smooth and glossy. Season to taste with salt and pepper.

Light Chicken Gravy with Thyme

Jus de poulet au thym

This is the best possible light gravy to accompany roast poultry. It is also good with fresh pasta, salsify à la meunière, leaf spinach, or braised Belgian endive. I adore thyme and, depending on the intensity of its flavor, which varies according to the season, I may use more or less for this recipe.

Serves 6
PREPARATION TIME: 15 MINUTES
COOKING TIME: 45–60 MINUTES

Ingredients:
3 TABLESPOONS PEANUT OIL
2 1/4 POUNDS CHICKEN WINGS, COARSELY CHOPPED
1 CUP CHOPPED CARROTS
2/3 CUP CHOPPED ONIONS
1 CUP DRY WHITE WINE
1 QUART COLD WATER
5 JUNIPER BERRIES, CRUSHED
1 GARLIC CLOVE, CRUSHED
A BUNCH OF THYME, PREFERABLY FRESH
SALT AND FRESHLY GROUND PEPPER

Heat the oil in a deep frying pan, put in the chicken wings, and fry over high heat until golden brown, stirring occasionally with a wooden spoon. Pour off the oil and the fat released by the chicken, then add the carrots and onions. Stir with a wooden spoon and sweat gently for 3 minutes. Pour in the white wine and reduce the liquid by half. Add all the other ingredients, being sparing with the salt and pepper, and bubble the sauce gently for 45 minutes, skimming as often as necessary. Pass it through a conical sieve; it is now ready to serve. For a more concentrated flavor, reduce the sauce over medium heat.

The sauce will keep in an airtight container in the refrigerator for several days, or for several weeks in the freezer.

Chasseur Sauce

Sauce chasseur

This light, savory sauce is quick to make. It goes very well with poultry and veal.

Serves 8
PREPARATION TIME: 10 MINUTES
COOKING TIME: ABOUT 20 MINUTES

Ingredients:
7 TABLESPOONS BUTTER
3 CUPS THINLY SLICED BUTTON MUSHROOMS
1/3 CUP MINCED SHALLOT
1 3/4 CUPS DRY WHITE WINE
1 3/4 CUPS VEAL STOCK (PAGE 16)
1 TABLESPOON SNIPPED FLAT-LEAF PARSLEY
1 TEASPOON SNIPPED TARRAGON
SALT AND FRESHLY GROUND BLACK PEPPER

Heat half the butter in a shallow pan, add the mushrooms, and cook over medium heat for 1 minute. Add the shallot and cook for 1 more minute, taking care not to let it color.

Tip the mushroom and shallot mixture into a fine-mesh conical sieve to drain off the cooking butter. Put them back into the shallow pan, add the wine, and reduce it by half over medium heat. Pour in the veal stock and cook gently for 10–15 minutes, until the sauce is thick enough to coat the back of a spoon.

Take the pan off the heat and whisk in the remaining butter and the snipped herbs. Season to taste with salt and pepper.

CHICKEN WITH CHASSEUR SAUCE

Périgueux Sauce

Sauce Périgueux

This sauce is excellent served with little hot pies or pâtés en croûte, with beef tournedos, or pan-fried saddle of lamb, and, of course, on pasta. To make the sauce richer and more unctuous, whisk in $^1/_4$ cup foie-gras butter (page 63) just before serving, but omit the chilled butter.

USE THE JUICE FROM FRESHLY
COOKED PRESERVED TRUFFLES

Serves 6
PREPARATION TIME: 5 MINUTES
COOKING TIME: ABOUT 30 MINUTES

Ingredients:
$1^3/_4$ CUPS VEAL STOCK (PAGE 16)
$^1/_4$ CUP BOTTLED TRUFFLE JUICE, OR (PREFERABLY)
THE COOKING JUICE FROM FRESH TRUFFLES
2 TABLESPOONS MINCED TRUFFLES
$1^1/_2$ TABLESPOONS BUTTER, CHILLED AND DICED
SALT AND FRESHLY GROUND PEPPER

In a small saucepan, reduce the veal stock over medium heat (1) until it forms a veil and lightly coats the back of a spoon (2). Add the truffle juice (3) and cook for 5 minutes longer. Add the minced truffles (4) and give the sauce a bubble. Take the pan off the heat and add the butter, one piece at a time, swirling and rotating the pan to incorporate it (5). Season the sauce with salt and pepper to taste, and serve immediately (6).

PÉRIGOURDINE SAUCE: You can replace the chopped truffles with truffles sliced into disks or "turned" into olive shapes. The sauce is then known as *Périgourdine.*

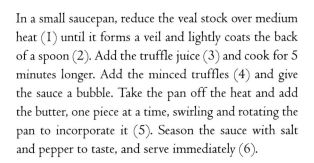

MINCE THE TRUFFLES

Charcutière Sauce

Sauce charcutière

A memory from my childhood... This homey sauce accompanied the pork chops and mashed potatoes that our grandfather and father served to the customers at their charcuterie in Charolles. If there was any left over, they would serve it to us the next day with a dish of wide noodles.

I prefer this rather piquant sauce to have a slightly thick consistency, which I think complements the texture of pork.

Serves 4
PREPARATION TIME: 5 MINUTES
COOKING TIME: ABOUT 20 MINUTES

Ingredients:
2 TABLESPOONS BUTTER
1/4 CUP MINCED ONIONS
1/2 CUP DRY WHITE WINE
1 1/4 CUPS VEAL STOCK (PAGE 16)
1 TABLESPOON STRONG DIJON MUSTARD
3 TABLESPOONS BEURRE MANIÉ (PAGE 31)
2-3 CORNICHONS, CUT IN LONG, THIN STRIPS
SALT AND FRESHLY GROUND PEPPER

TO MAKE A BEURRE MANIÉ, MASH BUTTER AND FLOUR WITH A FORK

ADD THE VEAL STOCK

In a small saucepan, melt the butter, add the onions, and sweat gently for 1 minute without coloring. Pour in the wine and reduce by half over medium heat. Add the veal stock and bubble the sauce gently until it is thick enough to coat the back of a spoon. Whisk in the mustard and the *beurre manié,* a little at a time, and cook for 2 minutes longer. Season to taste with salt and pepper. Pass the sauce through a conical sieve into a small saucepan containing the cornichons and serve it immediately, or keep it warm for a few minutes in a *bain-marie* set over low heat.

POUR THE WINE OVER THE ONIONS

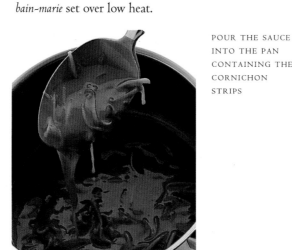

POUR THE SAUCE INTO THE PAN CONTAINING THE CORNICHON STRIPS

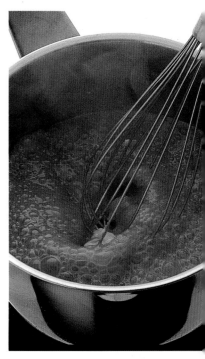

WHISK IN THE MUSTARD AND THE BEURRE MANIÉ

Light Lamb Gravy Scented with Lavender Honey

Jus d'agneau au parfum de miel de lavande

This is a lovely sauce to serve with grilled lamb chops or a roast leg of lamb. Or do as we did as children — make a well in the middle of a pile of mashed potatoes and pour in a few spoonfuls of gravy.

Serves 8
PREPARATION TIME: 15 MINUTES
COOKING TIME: 1 HOUR 15 MINUTES

Ingredients:
1/4 CUP PEANUT OIL
2 1/4 POUNDS NECK OF LAMB ON THE BONE, COARSELY CHOPPED
2 HEAPED TABLESPOONS HONEY, PREFERABLY LAVENDER
1 CUP COARSELY CHOPPED CARROTS
2/3 CUP COARSELY CHOPPED ONIONS
1 CUP RED WINE
5 CUPS WATER
1 BOUQUET GARNI (PAGE 10)
6 PEPPERCORNS, CRUSHED
1 RIPE TOMATO, PEELED, SEEDED, AND CHOPPED
1 GARLIC CLOVE, CRUSHED
SALT AND FRESHLY GROUND PEPPER

Heat the oil in a deep frying pan, put in the lamb, and fry briskly until browned all over. Pour off the oil and the fat released by the lamb. Using a metal spatula, spread the honey over the pieces of lamb, then add the carrot and onion to the pan. Stir with a wooden spoon and sweat gently for 3 minutes. Deglaze with the red wine and cook over medium heat for 5 minutes. Add the rest of the ingredients, being sparing with the salt and pepper, and bubble the sauce gently for 1 hour, skimming the surface whenever necessary. Pass it through a conical sieve; it is now ready to serve, but for a more concentrated aroma, reduce the sauce for a little longer.

The sauce will keep in an airtight container in the refrigerator for a few days, or for several weeks in the freezer.

Orange Sauce

Sauce bigarade

I love this sauce served with slices of pan-fried calf's liver or sliced broiled kidneys. For a classic sauce for duck à l'orange, I add some duck wings (when I can get them), which I brown quickly before adding them to the sauce along with the veal stock at the beginning of cooking.

Serves 6
PREPARATION TIME: 10 MINUTES
COOKING TIME: ABOUT 50 MINUTES

Ingredients:
1/4 CUP SUGAR
3 TABLESPOONS RED WINE VINEGAR
3 CUPS VEAL STOCK (PAGE 16)
JUICE OF 3 ORANGES
ZEST OF 2 ORANGES, CUT IN FINE JULIENNE AND BLANCHED
3/4 POUND DUCK WINGS (OPTIONAL)
JUICE OF 1 LEMON
ZEST OF 1 LEMON, CUT IN FINE JULIENNE AND BLANCHED
SALT AND FRESHLY GROUND PEPPER

Put the sugar and vinegar in a deep frying pan and cook over a very low heat to make a deep golden caramel. Immediately pour in the veal stock and orange and lemon juices and bring to a boil. (Add the browned duck wings, if using.) Lower the heat and cook gently for 45 minutes, skimming the surface whenever necessary. The sauce should now be thick enough to coat the back of a spoon lightly. If it is not, cook for a little longer. Pass the sauce through a conical sieve, season to taste with salt and pepper, add the orange and lemon zests, and serve. If you are not serving the sauce immediately, keep it warm in a *bain-marie* without adding the zests and add them only at the last moment.

Bordelaise Sauce

Sauce bordelaise

This wonderful sauce looks as good as it tastes. It is delectable with any cut of beef, such as entrecôte, ribs, or sirloin. Personally, I add double the quantity of beef marrow, which I absolutely adore.

Serves 4
PREPARATION TIME: 10 MINUTES
COOKING TIME: ABOUT 30 MINUTES

Ingredients:
1/3 CUP MINCED SHALLOTS
8 WHITE PEPPERCORNS, CRUSHED
I CUP RED BORDEAUX WINE
I1/4 CUPS VEAL STOCK (PAGE 16)
I SMALL BOUQUET GARNI (PAGE 10)
1/2 POUND BEEF MARROW, SOAKED IN ICE WATER FOR
4 HOURS
2 TABLESPOONS BUTTER, CHILLED AND DICED
SALT AND FRESHLY GROUND PEPPER

Put the shallot, crushed peppercorns, and wine in a saucepan, set over high heat, and reduce the wine by one-third. Add the veal stock and bouquet garni and bubble gently for about 20 minutes, or until the sauce will coat the back of a spoon. Pass it through a wire-mesh conical sieve into another saucepan.

Drain the beef marrow and cut it into small pieces or rounds. Place in a small saucepan, cover with a little cold water, and salt lightly. Set over medium heat and bring to a boil. Immediately remove from the heat, leave the marrow for 30 seconds, and then drain it gently.

Season the sauce with salt and pepper to taste, whisk in the butter, add the well-drained beef marrow, and serve immediately.

Eggplant Sauce with Tarragon

Sauce aubergine à l'estragon

The tarragon and mustard add a refreshing note to this sauce, while the eggplant makes it smooth and creamy. Serve it with roast rabbit, veal, or pork chops. It also makes an excellent accompaniment to a dish of wide noodles.

Serves 4
PREPARATION TIME: 10 MINUTES
COOKING TIME: ABOUT 25 MINUTES

Ingredients:
2 CUPS EGGPLANT, UNPEELED, CUT IN CUBES
2 TABLESPOONS OLIVE OIL
1/2 CUP MINCED SHALLOTS
1/4 CUP RED WINE
I1/4 CUPS VEAL STOCK (PAGE 16)
2 TABLESPOONS HEAVY CREAM
A LARGE PINCH OF PAPRIKA
I TABLESPOON WHOLEGRAIN MUSTARD
I TABLESPOON SNIPPED TARRAGON
SALT

Lightly salt the eggplant cubes, leave for 5 minutes to remove any bitterness, and pat dry with paper towel. Heat the oil in a saucepan and put in the shallot and cubes of eggplant. Cook over medium heat, stirring with a wooden spoon, until the eggplant begins to soften. Add the red wine and cook for 3 minutes, still over medium heat. Pour in the veal stock and bubble gently for 15 minutes. Add the cream and a generous pinch of paprika, then transfer the sauce to a blender and whizz for 30 seconds.

Pass the sauce through a wire-mesh conical sieve into another saucepan, add the mustard and tarragon, and bring back to a boil. Season to taste with salt, and serve at once.

Peach Sauce

Sauce aux pêches

I serve this delicate, fruity sauce with my pigeonneau de Bresse rôti aux pêches or with a young duckling. For preference, make the sauce with white peaches.

Serves 4
PREPARATION TIME: 10 MINUTES
COOKING TIME: ABOUT 45 MINUTES

Ingredients:
2 TABLESPOONS BUTTER
2 1/2 TABLESPOONS SUGAR
2 VERY RIPE MEDIUM PEACHES, PEELED AND
CUT IN CUBES
1 1/2 TABLESPOONS COGNAC
3 TABLESPOONS RED WINE VINEGAR
1/2 CUP RED WINE, PREFERABLY BURGUNDY
1 CLOVE
1 TABLESPOON FENNEL SEEDS
1 1/4 CUPS VEAL STOCK (PAGE 16)
1 1/2 TABLESPOONS BUTTER, CHILLED AND DICED
SALT AND FRESHLY GROUND PEPPER

Melt the butter in a deep frying pan, add the sugar, and stir with a wooden spoon. As soon as the sugar has caramelized and begun to color lightly, put in the peach cubes and increase the heat. Cook, stirring continuously, until the peaches have almost collapsed into a purée. Add the cognac and then, after 30 seconds, the vinegar. After 1 more minute, pour in the wine and add the clove and fennel seeds.

Bring to a boil and cook gently for 10 minutes, skimming the surface with a slotted spoon as necessary. Pour in the veal stock and cook the sauce for about 30 minutes, until it coats the back of a spoon. Pass it through a conical sieve, whisk in the chilled butter, a little at a time, season to taste, and serve immediately.

Zingara Sauce

Sauce zingara

Serve this fine, delicate sauce with pan-fried or broiled poultry or with veal cutlets, chops, or scaloppine.

Serves 6
PREPARATION TIME: 10 MINUTES
COOKING TIME: ABOUT 35 MINUTES

Ingredients:
1 3/4 CUPS VEAL STOCK (PAGE 16)
1 TABLESPOON COOKED TOMATO COULIS (PAGE 66)
2 TABLESPOONS BUTTER
3/4 CUP BUTTON MUSHROOMS, CUT IN *BATONS*
1/4 CUP DRY WHITE WINE
1/4 CUP LEAN HAM, CUT IN *BATONS*
1/4 CUP COOKED TONGUE, CUT IN *BATONS*
1/4 CUP FRESH OR PRESERVED TRUFFLE, CUT IN
BATONS
2 TABLESPOONS BEST-QUALITY MADEIRA
SALT AND CAYENNE

Put the veal stock and tomato coulis in a saucepan and reduce by two-thirds over medium heat, then pass the liquid through a wire-mesh conical sieve into a bowl. Set aside.

In another saucepan, melt the butter, add the mushrooms, and sweat them gently for 30 seconds. Pour in the white wine and reduce it almost completely. Add the ham, tongue, and truffle and mix delicately with a wooden spoon, then pour in the Madeira and cook at a bare simmer for 2 minutes. Add the reduced veal stock and simmer for 5 minutes longer. Season the sauce to taste with salt and cayenne, and serve at once.

PEEL THE MANGO AND CUT THE FLESH
FROM THE PIT

Exotic Sauce

Sauce exotique

This fruity, refreshing sauce has a light spiciness. It is particularly good with sautéed chicken or rabbit, accompanied by some leaf spinach or fresh pasta.

Serves 4
PREPARATION TIME: 5 MINUTES
COOKING TIME: ABOUT 15 MINUTES

Ingredients:
1 VERY RIPE MANGO
2 PASSION FRUIT
2 TABLESPOONS COGNAC OR ARMAGNAC
1 CUP VEAL STOCK (PAGE 16)
1/2 CUP HEAVY CREAM
4 DROPS OF HOT-PEPPER SAUCE
SALT AND FRESHLY GROUND PEPPER

Using a small knife with a flexible blade, peel the mango and cut the flesh from the pit. Finely dice the flesh and place in a small saucepan. Halve the passion fruit, scoop the seeds into the saucepan, and add the cognac or Armagnac. Cook the exotic fruit mixture over low heat for 5 minutes, then add the veal stock and cook for another 5 minutes. Pour in the cream, add the hot-pepper sauce, and bubble the sauce for 5 minutes, then transfer to a blender and whizz for 1 minute. Pass the sauce through a wire-mesh conical sieve into a small saucepan, season to taste with salt and pepper, and serve immediately, or keep it warm for a few minutes in a *bain-marie*.

HALVE THE PASSION FRUIT AND SCOOP
OUT THE SEEDS

ADD THE COLD
VEAL STOCK

ADD THE HOT-PEPPE
SAUCE

PURÉE THE SAUCE
IN A BLENDER

Juniper Sauce

Sauce au genièvre

This sauce is simple but highly scented, with a hint of muskiness. It is perfect with grilled or pan-fried steaks or lightly cooked game, such as pan-fried fillets of rabbit or medallions of venison.

Serves 6
PREPARATION TIME: 5 MINUTES
COOKING TIME: ABOUT 25 MINUTES

Ingredients:
$^1/_3$ CUP CHOPPED SHALLOTS
I CUP RED WINE, PREFERABLY CÔTES DU RHÔNE
I$^1/_4$ CUPS VEAL STOCK (PAGE 16)
14 JUNIPER BERRIES, CRUSHED
2 TABLESPOONS RED-CURRANT JELLY
3 TABLESPOONS BUTTER, CHILLED AND DICED
SALT AND FRESHLY GROUND PEPPER

Put the shallot and wine in a saucepan, set over medium heat, and reduce the wine by one-third. Add the veal stock, then the juniper berries and bubble gently for 15 minutes. Stir in the red-currant jelly and, as soon as it has dissolved, pass the sauce through a wire-mesh conical sieve into a clean pan. Whisk in the butter, a little at a time, season to taste with salt and pepper, and serve immediately.

Bolognaise Sauce

Sauce bolognaise

I love this sauce served with a thick potato purée, braised white cabbage, pan-fried turkey scallops, and, of course, its classic partner, spaghetti.

Serves 8
PREPARATION TIME: 10 MINUTES
COOKING TIME: ABOUT 40 MINUTES

Ingredients:
$^1/_4$ CUP PEANUT OIL
I POUND BEEF OR LAMB, FRESHLY GROUND
$^1/_2$ CUP CHOPPED ONION
I MEDIUM GARLIC CLOVE, MINCED
I SMALL BOUQUET GARNI (PAGE 10), INCLUDING A
SPRIG OF ROSEMARY
I$^1/_4$ CUPS COOKED TOMATO COULIS (PAGE 66)
I$^1/_4$ CUPS VEAL STOCK (PAGE 16)
3 TABLESPOONS BUTTER, CHILLED AND DICED
I TABLESPOON CHOPPED PARSLEY
SALT AND FRESHLY GROUND PEPPER

In a frying pan, heat 3 tablespoons of the oil and, when it is very hot, add the ground meat. Brown it all over, stirring with a wooden spoon. Immediately tip it into a colander and leave for 30 seconds to drain off the cooking fat.

Put the remaining oil in a saucepan, add the onions, and sweat them gently for 30 seconds without coloring. Add the meat, garlic, bouquet garni, tomato coulis, and veal stock and bring to a boil. Immediately lower the heat and simmer the sauce gently for 35 minutes, stirring every 5–10 minutes with a wooden spoon. Remove the bouquet garni, and beat the butter into the sauce with the wooden spoon, a little at a time. Season with salt and plenty of pepper, and stir in the parsley just before serving.

Devil Sauce

Sauce diable

I often use this robust, highly scented sauce, which goes very well with all grilled poultry, particularly spatchcocked poussin or chicken.

Serves 4
PREPARATION TIME: 5 MINUTES
COOKING TIME: ABOUT 45 MINUTES

Ingredients:
2 TABLESPOONS BEST-QUALITY RED WINE VINEGAR
1/2 CUP DRY WHITE WINE
20 WHITE PEPPERCORNS, CRUSHED
1/3 CUP CHOPPED SHALLOTS
I BOUQUET GARNI (PAGE 10),
INCLUDING 2 SPRIGS OF TARRAGON
1 3/4 CUPS VEAL STOCK (PAGE 16)
3 TABLESPOONS BUTTER, CHILLED AND DICED
I TABLESPOON SNIPPED CHERVIL OR FLAT-LEAF
PARSLEY
SALT AND FRESHLY GROUND PEPPER

Combine the vinegar, white wine, crushed white peppercorns, shallot, and bouquet garni in a saucepan. Set over medium heat and reduce the liquid by four-fifths. Pour in the veal stock and bubble gently for about 20 minutes, or until the sauce is thick enough to coat the back of a spoon. Pass it through a wire-mesh sieve into a clean saucepan and whisk in the butter, a little at a time. Season to taste with salt and pepper, and add the chervil or parsley just before serving.

Light Chicken Sauce with Curaçao

Sauce volaille au Curaçao

This sauce has a very light consistency, almost like a thin gravy. I like to serve it with roast or pan-fried poussin or squab. You can accentuate the Curaçao flavor by adding a touch more of the liqueur.

Serves 4
PREPARATION TIME: 5 MINUTES
COOKING TIME: ABOUT 30 MINUTES

Ingredients:
2 TABLESPOONS PEANUT OIL
1/2 POUND CHICKEN WINGS AND NECKS, BLANCHED,
REFRESHED, AND DRAINED
1/2 CUP DICED SHALLOTS
3/4 CUP DICED CARROTS
1/2 CUP DICED CELERY
4 STAR ANISE, COARSELY CHOPPED
2 TABLESPOONS CURAÇAO
I CUP CHICKEN STOCK (PAGE 18)
I CUP VEAL STOCK (PAGE 16)
2 TABLESPOONS BUTTER, CHILLED AND DICED
SALT AND FRESHLY GROUND PEPPER

Heat the oil in a deep frying pan, put in the chicken wings and necks, and quickly brown them all over. Pour off the oil and fat rendered by the chicken, then add the diced vegetables to the chicken in the pan, together with the star anise, and sweat everything gently for 2 minutes.

Add the Curaçao and cook for I minute. Pour in the chicken stock, increase the heat to high, and reduce the stock by half. Add the veal stock and simmer the sauce gently for 20 minutes longer. Pass it through a wire-mesh conical sieve into a clean pan, whisk in the butter a little at a time, season to taste with salt and pepper, and serve immediately.

Cherry Tomato Sauce

Sauce aux petites tomates cerises

This sauce is delicious served not only with pasta, but also with many grilled white meats. I greedily sup it with a spoon. It can be reheated very successfully and will keep in an airtight container in the refrigerator for several days.

Serves 8
PREPARATION TIME: 15 MINUTES
COOKING TIME: ABOUT 1 HOUR

Ingredients:
2 1/4 POUNDS VERY RIPE CHERRY TOMATOES, STEMS REMOVED
1 TEASPOON SUGAR
1 TABLESPOON SNIPPED BASIL LEAVES
2 TABLESPOONS RUBY PORT WINE
3 TABLESPOONS OLIVE OIL
1/3 CUP CHOPPED ONIONS
2/3 CUP CHOPPED CELERY
6 THICK SLICES OF BACON (ABOUT 1/4 POUND), DICED
6 DROPS OF HOT-PEPPER SAUCE
1 TEASPOON WORCESTERSHIRE SAUCE
JUICE OF 1/2 LEMON
SALT AND FRESHLY GROUND PEPPER

Preheat the oven to 320°F.

Put the tomatoes into an earthenware or enamel casserole with a lid and add the sugar, basil, port wine, and a little salt. Cover and cook in the oven for about 45 minutes, until the tomatoes have collapsed into a purée.

Meanwhile, combine the olive oil, onion, celery, and bacon in a saucepan and set over medium heat. Cook for about 20 minutes, stirring frequently with a wooden spoon, until everything is pale golden and well softened. Spoon off the excess oil, then mix the contents of the saucepan with the tomatoes. Transfer to a blender and whizz for 1 minute. Pass the sauce through a wire-mesh conical sieve into another saucepan and add the hot-pepper sauce, Worcestershire sauce, lemon juice, and salt and pepper to taste. Simmer the sauce for 5 minutes longer, then serve immediately.

Savory and Tapenade Sauce

Sauce sarriette et tapenade

This sauce is very fluid, almost like a jus, and bursting with the Provençal flavors of savory and olives. I often serve it with pan-fried or roast shoulder or leg of lamb. If you happen to have some lamb stock, substitute it for the veal stock.

Serves 4
PREPARATION TIME: 5 MINUTES
COOKING TIME: ABOUT 25 MINUTES

Ingredients:
1/2 CUP DRY WHITE WINE
1/3 CUP CHOPPED SHALLOT
1/3 CUP SAVORY
6 WHITE PEPPERCORNS, CRUSHED
1 CUP VEAL STOCK (PAGE 16)
1/4 CUP BLACK OR GREEN TAPENADE (OLIVE PASTE)
2 TABLESPOONS BUTTER, CHILLED AND DICED
SALT AND FRESHLY GROUND PEPPER

Combine the wine, shallot, savory, and crushed peppercorns in a small saucepan, set over medium heat, and reduce the wine by half. Pour in the veal stock, reduce the heat to very low, and simmer gently for 20 minutes. Whisk in the tapenade. Then, still over the lowest possible heat, whisk in the butter, a little at a time. Season the sauce with salt and pepper, pass it through a wire-mesh conical sieve, and serve at once.

Curry Sauce

Sauce au curry

Serve this creamy, slightly fruity sauce with broiled veal scallops or chicken, garnished with curried or pilaff rice. The quantity of curry powder can be varied to suit your own taste.

Serves 8
PREPARATION TIME: 10 MINUTES
COOKING TIME: ABOUT 30 MINUTES

Ingredients:
3 TABLESPOONS BUTTER
$1/3$ CUP CHOPPED ONIONS
2 CUPS PINEAPPLE, CUT IN SMALL PIECES
1 MEDIUM BANANA, CUT IN ROUNDS
1 APPLE, WASHED AND CUT IN SMALL PIECES
$1/3$ CUP CURRY POWDER
2 TABLESPOONS GRATED FRESH OR DRIED COCONUT
$1 1/4$ CUPS VEAL STOCK (PAGE 16)
1 CUP COCONUT MILK
SALT

Melt the butter in a saucepan, add the onions, and sweat them over low heat for 1 minute. Add the pineapple, banana, and apple and cook gently for 5 minutes, stirring with a wooden spoon. Add the curry and grated coconut, then pour in the veal stock and coconut milk. Bring to a boil and bubble the sauce gently for 20 minutes. Pass it through a wire-mesh conical sieve, season with salt to taste, and serve immediately. If you wish, you can keep the sauce warm in a *bain-marie*; dot the surface with a few flakes of butter to prevent a skin from forming.

Five-Spice Sauce

Sauce aux cinq épices

This sauce is excellent with a chicken baked in a salt crust, or with pan-fried veal medallions served with pilaff rice.

Serves 4
PREPARATION TIME: 20 MINUTES
COOKING TIME: ABOUT 30 MINUTES

Ingredients:
$1/2$ POUND CHICKEN WINGS, BLANCHED,
REFRESHED, AND DRAINED
2 TABLESPOONS PEANUT OIL
$1/2$ CUP CHOPPED CARROTS
$1/3$ CUP CHOPPED ONIONS
$1/4$ CUP WHITE WINE VINEGAR
$1 3/4$ CUPS CHICKEN STOCK (PAGE 18)
$1/2$ CUP CHOPPED TOMATOES, PEELED AND SEEDED
1 SMALL BOUQUET GARNI (PAGE 10),
INCLUDING A SPRIG OF TARRAGON
$1/2$ CUP HEAVY CREAM
1 TEASPOON FIVE-SPICE POWDER
SALT AND FRESHLY GROUND PEPPER

Put the chicken wings and oil in a deep frying pan and brown over high heat. Pour off the oil and fat from the chicken, then add the carrots and onions to the pan and sweat them for 2 minutes. Off the heat, sprinkle on the vinegar and leave for 1 minute. Add the chicken stock, tomatoes, and bouquet garni and bring to a boil, then cook over low heat, skimming the surface whenever necessary, until the sauce lightly coats the back of a spoon. Add the cream and five-spice powder and bubble gently for 2 minutes. Pass the sauce through a wire-mesh conical sieve and season to taste. Keep it warm in a *bain-marie* or serve immediately.

ADD THE ONIONS AND
CARROTS TO THE PAN

SPRINKLE IN THE VINEGAR

COOK UNTIL THE SAUCE
LIGHTLY COATS THE BACK
OF THE SPOON

ADD THE FIVE-SPICE POWDER

Choose the sauce for a dessert according to the main ingredient. As with savory dishes, the purpose of the sauce is to accompany the principle ingredient but never to dominate it. Remember that the dessert comes at the end of the meal; being the last dish, it creates the final and lasting impression, so it must be perfect.

Dessert Sauces

The star of this chapter is crème anglaise, *the most famous, classic, and well-loved sweet sauce, which sadly is also one of the most ill-used and badly executed.* Crème anglaise *should be like a perfect hollandaise — creamy, unctuous, rich yet delicate, with a superb mouth feel; then I adore it, supping it up with a spoon like soup. But when it is watery, insipid, and depressingly unsatisfying on the palate, I cannot swallow it. This is why I have made my recipe as explicit as possible, by means of clear step-by-step photographic instructions. Apart from the classic addition of vanilla, the sauce can be scented with many other flavorings to make it shine like a beacon.*

Fruit coulis are deliciously refreshing, with bright glowing colors and flavors ranging from sweet to bitter or acid, depending on the fruit used. They can be enhanced with a touch of spice. Stored in airtight containers, they will keep very well in the refrigerator for several days.

Bear in mind that you should never serve more than one or two coulis on the same plate with fruits or a dessert. Each one has its own distinctive flavor which could be diametrically opposed to another. To maintain the harmony of flavors and aromas, avoid the temptation to combine a riot of different colors on the plate; this will only spoil your dessert.

Chocolate sauces should be served at the right temperature (between 86° and 104°F) and made with the finest quality chocolate for the best results.

Many dessert sauces and coulis are delicious served with ice creams and sorbets. What could be more divine than vanilla or pistachio ice cream coated with warm chocolate sauce?

POACHED PEARS WITH
BLACKBERRY COULIS

Stock Syrup

Sirop à sorbet ou coulis de fruits

This basic syrup (30° on the Beaumé scale or 1.2624 density) is used with fresh fruits to make fruit sorbets and coulis which can accompany any number of desserts.

Makes about 3 cups
PREPARATION TIME: 5 MINUTES
COOKING TIME: ABOUT 7 MINUTES

Ingredients:
2 CUPS SUGAR
1 1/2 CUPS COLD WATER
2 OUNCES LIQUID GLUCOSE

Combine the sugar, water, and glucose in a saucepan and bring slowly to a boil over low heat, stirring continuously with a wooden spoon. Boil for 3 minutes, skimming the surface if necessary. Pass the syrup through a wire-mesh conical sieve and leave to cool before refrigerating.

Stock syrup will keep in an airtight container in the refrigerator for up to 2 weeks.

Blackberry Coulis

Coulis de mûres

This divine coulis can accompany almost all charlottes, whatever their flavor. It is equally delicious served with parfaits or iced bombes, or ice creams such as coconut, vanilla, or banana. Like all coulis, it will keep well for several days in an airtight container in the refrigerator.

Serves 8
PREPARATION TIME: 5 MINUTES

Ingredients:
2 1/2 CUPS RIPE BLACKBERRIES, HULLED
1/4 CUP KIRSCH
2/3 CUP STOCK SYRUP (LEFT)
JUICE OF 1/2 LEMON

Put all the ingredients in a blender and whizz for about 1 minute, until puréed. Rub the sauce through a wire-mesh conical sieve and serve cold.

(Picture page 156)

Grapefruit Coulis with Mint

Coulis de pamplemousse à la menthe

This refreshing coulis marries well with orange desserts, chocolate charlotte, or black-currant sorbet. It looks very attractive if you scatter on a few mint leaves snipped as finely as possible just before serving.

Serves 6
PREPARATION TIME: 5 MINUTES

Ingredients:
2 GRAPEFRUIT, PREFERABLY PINK, EACH ABOUT 1 POUND
1/4 CUP FRESH MINT, SNIPPED
3 1/2 TABLESPOONS SUGAR
2/3 CUP PLAIN YOGURT
5 TEASPOONS VODKA

Using a knife with a flexible blade, peel the grapefruit, removing all pith and membrane, and cut each one into six. Place in a blender with the mint and sugar, whizz for 1 minute, and pass through a wire-mesh conical sieve into a mixing bowl. Whisk in the yogurt, then mix in the vodka. Serve very cold.

Coulis of Pears with Red Wine

Coulis de poires au vin rouge

Serve this powerful and delicious coulis with an iced vacherin, a Saint-Honoré filled with whipped cream with an accompaniment of red berries, or with a simple compote of fresh apricots. The coulis will keep well for several days in an airtight container in the refrigerator.

Serves 6
PREPARATION TIME: 10 MINUTES,
PLUS 30 MINUTES' MARINATING

Ingredients:
3 VERY RIPE PEARS, EACH ABOUT 7 OUNCES
A PINCH OF GROUND CINNAMON
1/2 CUP RED WINE, PREFERABLY BORDEAUX
2 TABLESPOONS COLD WATER
JUICE OF 1/2 LEMON
3/4 CUP SUGAR

Peel and core the pears. Cut them into small pieces and place in a bowl with the cinnamon and red wine. Cover with plastic wrap and leave to marinate for 30 minutes.

Combine the water, lemon juice, and sugar in a thick-bottomed saucepan. Heat the mixture over very low heat and bubble it gently until it becomes a pale caramel. Take the pan off the heat and pour in the red wine in which you marinated the pears. (Be careful not to get splashed as the cold wine hits the hot caramel.) After 5 minutes, stir the diluted and cooled caramel with a wooden spoon, then pour it over the pears. Transfer to a blender and whizz for 1 minute, then chill the coulis before serving. If it becomes too thick, dilute it with 2 or 3 spoons of cold water.

TOP RIGHT:
WARM PLUM TART WITH
ORANGE BUTTER

Orange Butter

Beurre à l'orange

This is delicious served with crêpes, lemon charlotte, a warm plum tart, or a chocolate soufflé. A few drops of Grand Marnier or Curaçao add extra warmth to the sauce in winter.

Serves 6
PREPARATION TIME: 5 MINUTES
COOKING TIME: ABOUT 5 MINUTES

Ingredients:
JUICE OF 6 ORANGES, EACH ABOUT 1/2 POUND,
STRAINED THROUGH A CONICAL SIEVE
1/2 CUP + 6 TABLESPOONS CONFECTIONERS' SUGAR
9 TABLESPOONS BUTTER, SOFTENED TO A PASTE

Put the orange juice and sugar in a saucepan and reduce by half over medium heat. Remove from the heat and whisk in the softened butter, a little at a time. Serve the sauce at room temperature.

❶ ❷
❸ ❹

Crème Anglaise

Crème anglaise *(custard sauce) can accompany any number of cold desserts. For a light, foamy, unctuous sauce to serve with a hot dessert like apple charlotte, warm rice pudding, or chocolate soufflé, warm the custard slightly and add a little Grand Marnier, champagne, or other alcohol, then whizz it in a blender for 30 seconds.* Crème anglaise *can also be churned to make the ever-popular vanilla ice cream.*

Makes about 3 cups
PREPARATION TIME: 15 MINUTES
COOKING TIME: ABOUT 5 MINUTES

Ingredients:
6 EGG YOLKS
$^1/_2$ CUP + 2 TABLESPOONS SUGAR
2 CUPS MILK
1 VANILLA BEAN, SPLIT LENGTHWISE

ADD MELTED CHOCOLATE
FOR A CHOCOLATE CRÈME
ANGLAISE

In a bowl, whisk the egg yolks with one-third of the sugar (1) until the mixture is pale and has a ribbon consistency (2). Put the milk, vanilla, and the remaining sugar in a saucepan (3) and stir with a whisk for a few seconds, then bring to a boil. Pour the boiling milk onto the egg yolks, whisking continuously (4). Return the mixture to the pan and cook gently, stirring with a wooden spoon, until the temperature of the custard reaches about 175°F. It should have thickened enough to coat the back of the wooden spoon and for your finger to leave a trail when you run it down the spoon.

Remove the vanilla bean and immediately pour the sauce into a clean bowl set in crushed ice to speed up the cooling process. Stir the custard occasionally with a wooden spoon to stop it from coagulating and prevent a skin from forming. Once it is completely cold, cover with plastic wrap and refrigerate for a minimum of 2 and a maximum of 48 hours.

COFFEE OR CHOCOLATE CRÈME ANGLAISE:
For a coffee or chocolate *crème anglaise*, replace the vanilla bean with 2 tablespoons instant coffee powder or 2 ounces melted bittersweet chocolate.

THE CUSTARD SAUCE
SHOULD COAT THE
BACK OF A SPOON

CHECK THE CONSISTENCY OF
THE CUSTARD SAUCE ON THE
BACK OF A WOODEN SPOON

Licorice Sauce

Sauce à la réglisse

This unusual sauce has a delicious flavor of licorice, which perfectly complements a pear tart, plum clafoutis, *pistachio ice cream, or a compote of yellow peaches.*

I add whipped cream just before serving to lighten and soften the sauce. Without the addition of the cream, it will keep in the refrigerator for 48 hours, covered with plastic wrap.

Serves 6
PREPARATION TIME: 15 MINUTES
COOKING TIME: ABOUT 5 MINUTES

Ingredients:
3 EGG YOLKS
1/3 CUP SUGAR
1 CUP MILK
2 OUNCES BLACK LICORICE STICKS,
CUT IN SMALL PIECES
1/4 CUP HEAVY CREAM, WHIPPED UNTIL FLOPPY

Follow the method for *crème anglaise* (page 161), substituting the licorice for the vanilla. Add the whipped cream just before serving.

Autumnal Sauce

Sauce automnale

This autumnal sauce is lovely with a compote of peaches or figs, or with baked apples.

Serves 8
PREPARATION TIME: 5 MINUTES
COOKING TIME: 10 MINUTES

Ingredients:
1 APPLE, ABOUT 4 OUNCES
2 MEDIUM BANANAS
JUICE OF 1 LEMON
2 HEAPING TABLESPOONS HONEY
SEEDS FROM 2 CARDAMOM PODS
1/2 CUP SUGAR
1 CUP WATER

Peel and core the apple and dice it finely. Peel the bananas and cut them in rounds.

Put the prepared fruits in a saucepan with the lemon juice, honey, cardamom seeds, sugar, and water and bring to a boil over low heat. Simmer very gently for 10 minutes, then pour into a blender and purée for 1 minute, or until very smooth. Pass the sauce through a conical sieve into a bowl. Leave at room temperature until cold, and refrigerate until ready to use.

Strawberry Coulis with Green Peppercorns

Coulis de fraises au poivre vert

I usually serve this coulis poured around a lemon sorbet, vanilla ice cream, or perhaps a poached pear or pear charlotte. Occasionally in summer I make amuse-gueules *of thinly sliced marinated raw tuna encircled by a ribbon of this refreshing sauce.*

Serves 8
PREPARATION TIME: 5 MINUTES

Ingredients:
1 1/2 PINTS VERY RIPE STRAWBERRIES, HULLED
1 1/2 TABLESPOONS SOFT GREEN BOTTLED
PEPPERCORNS, WELL DRAINED
1/2 CUP STOCK SYRUP (PAGE 158)
JUICE OF 1/2 LEMON
1 TABLESPOON POPPY SEEDS (OPTIONAL)

Put the strawberries, peppercorns, syrup, and lemon juice in a blender and whizz for 1 minute. Pass the coulis through a wire-mesh conical sieve and, if you wish, add the poppy seeds just before serving.

PUT THE STRAWBERRIES,
PEPPERCORNS, SYRUP, AND
LEMON JUICE INTO A BLENDER

RIGHT AND ABOVE: WHIZZ TO A
PURÉE FOR ABOUT 1 MINUTE

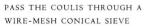

PASS THE COULIS THROUGH A
WIRE-MESH CONICAL SIEVE

ADD THE COFFEE TO THE
MAPLE SYRUP

WHISK IN THE ALCOHOL

Maple Syrup, Coffee, and Drambuie Sauce

Sauce café et Drambuie

This limpid, iridescent sauce is delicious served with a vanilla and praline parfait or with warm waffles. The alcohol adds an agreeable aroma, which is especially attractive in winter.

Serves 6
PREPARATION TIME: 5 MINUTES
COOKING TIME: ABOUT 2 MINUTES

Ingredients:
1 CUP MAPLE SYRUP
1 TABLESPOON INSTANT COFFEE, DISSOLVED
IN 1 TABLESPOON WATER
1/4 CUP VODKA
1/4 CUP DRAMBUIE
8 COFFEE BEANS, COARSELY CRUSHED

In a small saucepan, warm the maple syrup, then add the coffee. As soon as the syrup is hot but not boiling, take the pan off the heat and whisk in the vodka and Drambuie, not too vigorously. Cover the sauce with plastic wrap and keep in a cool place until cold. Stir in the crushed coffee beans just before serving.

WARM WAFFLES WITH
MAPLE SYRUP, COFFEE,
AND DRAMBUIE SAUCE

Prune and Armagnac Sauce

Sauce aux pruneaux et à l'Armagnac

This sauce is ideal in the fall, served with molded rice pudding, a hot soufflé of marrons glacés, pear or banana ice cream, and, of course, a prune clafoutis.

Serves 10
PREPARATION TIME: 10 MINUTES
COOKING TIME: ABOUT 30 MINUTES

Ingredients:
1/2 POUND PRUNES, PREFERABLY AGEN, SOAKED IN
COLD WATER FOR 6 HOURS
3/4 CUP SUGAR
1/2 CINNAMON STICK
2/3 CUP ARMAGNAC
1 CUP BUTTER

Drain the soaked prunes, place them in a saucepan with the sugar and cinnamon, and cover with cold water. Bring slowly to a boil over low heat and simmer for 20 minutes. Transfer to a bowl, remove the cinnamon, and leave the prunes to cool, then drain and pit them. Reserve the cooking syrup.

Cut six of the prunes into small, even pieces and reserve them in a bowl. Put the remaining prunes in a shallow pan with the Armagnac, 2/3 cup cooking syrup from the prunes, and 7 tablespoons butter and heat gently without boiling to about 140–158°F. Transfer to a blender and whizz for 1 minute. Scrape the puréed prunes into a saucepan and whisk in the remaining butter, a small piece at a time, and enough of the reserved syrup to give the sauce a light ribbon consistency. Add the prune pieces and serve the sauce tepid, or keep it in a *bain-marie* filled with not-too-hot water for a maximum of 30 minutes.

SIMMER THE HALVED PEACHES IN
THE SYRUP FOR 20 MINUTES

PURÉE THE PEACHES FOR 2
MINUTES TO MAKE A COULIS

White Peach Coulis with Star Anise

Coulis de pêches blanches à l'anis étoilé

This coulis is the perfect accompaniment for white peaches, either raw or lightly poached in syrup and served cold or warm. It is also excellent with wild strawberries or any delicate fruits.

Serves 8
PREPARATION TIME: 10 MINUTES
COOKING TIME: ABOUT 20 MINUTES

Ingredients:
2 VERY RIPE WHITE PEACHES
1 3/4 CUPS WATER
3/4 CUP SUGAR
4 STAR ANISE AND 2 CLOVES, TIED UP TOGETHER IN
A SQUARE OF CHEESECLOTH
JUICE OF 1 LEMON
2 ORANGES, PREFERABLY BLOOD ORANGES
1 TABLESPOON GRENADINE SYRUP (IF YOU ARE NOT
USING BLOOD ORANGES)

Put the peaches in a bowl, cover with boiling water, and leave for 15 seconds, then transfer to a bowl of cold water, using a slotted spoon. Skin and halve them with a sharp knife, leaving in the pits.

Place the halved peaches with their pits in a small saucepan. Add the water, sugar, star anise, cloves, and lemon juice, set over low heat, and bring to just below boiling point. Simmer for 20 minutes, then leave to cool at room temperature for 15 minutes.

Discard the peach pits and spices. Purée the contents of the pan in a blender for about 2 minutes, to make a coulis. Pass this through a fine-mesh conical strainer and keep in a cool place.

To make the orange syrup, squeeze the oranges and strain the juice into a small saucepan. Add the grenadine and reduce the juice over low heat until it becomes syrupy. Reserve it in a ramekin.

Pour the peach coulis around the fruits on individual plates and spoon a ribbon of orange syrup onto it. Using a toothpick or the tip of a knife, delicately swirl the syrup into the coulis.

RIGHT: SKIN THE
PEACHES BY POURING
ON BOILING WATER

SWIRL THE ORANGE SYRUP
INTO THE PEACH COULIS

TOSS THE SLICED BANANAS IN
LEMON JUICE

Honey Sauce

Sauce au miel

*This ambrosial sauce, lightly perfumed with honey, is delicious
with pancakes, crisp apple tartlets, French toast, and ice cream.*

Serves 8
PREPARATION TIME: 5 MINUTES
COOKING TIME: ABOUT 10 MINUTES

Ingredients:
1 1/3 CUPS SLICED RIPE BANANAS
JUICE OF 1 LEMON
1 1/4 CUPS STOCK SYRUP (PAGE 158)
2 TEASPOONS GROUND GINGER
3 TABLESPOONS HONEY

Immediately toss the bananas in the lemon juice. Put
them in a saucepan with the syrup, ginger, and honey
and boil for 5 minutes. Transfer to a blender and whizz
for 1 minute, then pass the sauce through a wire-mesh
conical sieve into a bowl. Stir until cold, cover with
plastic wrap, and refrigerate until ready to use.

PASS THE SAUCE
THROUGH A
WIRE-MESH
CONICAL SIEVE

PUT THEM IN A PAN WITH THE
SYRUP, GINGER, AND HONEY

Coffee Sabayon with Tia Maria

Sabayon au café Tia Maria

This sabayon is really a dessert in itself, but it also makes a delicious sauce for such desserts as gâteau de riz impératrice, apple tart, or pears poached in syrup.

Serves 4
PREPARATION TIME: 15–20 MINUTES
COOKING TIME: 15–20 MINUTES

Ingredients:
1/4 CUP COLD WATER
2 TABLESPOONS INSTANT COFFEE
1/4 CUP SUGAR
4 EGG YOLKS
1/4 CUP TIA MARIA

Half-fill with warm water a saucepan large enough to hold the base of a mixing bowl. Combine the cold water and coffee in the said bowl and whisk with a balloon whisk to dissolve the coffee. Still whisking, add all the other ingredients.

Stand the base of the bowl in the saucepan of water and set the pan over medium heat. Start whisking and continue to do so for 10–12 minutes. The temperature of the water in the saucepan must not exceed 195°F, or the *sabayon* will start to coagulate. It is ready when it reaches the consistency of egg whites beaten to soft peaks, with an unctuous, shiny, fluffy, and light texture and a temperature not exceeding 130°F. As soon as the *sabayon* is ready, stop whisking, spoon it into bowls, large glasses, or a sauceboat, and serve immediately.

Mint Sauce

Sauce à la menthe

This creamy, refreshing sauce is excellent served with orange and grapefruit sections or a gâteau fraisier, or as a substitute for crème anglaise to accompany floating islands.

Serves 4
PREPARATION TIME: 15 MINUTES
COOKING TIME: ABOUT 5 MINUTES

Ingredients:
1 CUP MILK
1/2 CUP + 2 TABLESPOONS SUGAR
1 CUP FRESH MINT
3 EGG YOLKS
1 TABLESPOON SNIPPED MINT LEAVES
A FEW DROPS OF GREEN PEPPERMINT SYRUP

Put the milk and 1/2 cup of the sugar into a saucepan and bring slowly to a boil over low heat. As soon as it boils, remove from the heat, add the mint, cover, and leave to infuse for 10 minutes.

Put the egg yolks and remaining sugar in a bowl and whisk to a foamy ribbon consistency. Pour the milk infusion onto the egg mixture, stirring all the time. Return the mixture to the saucepan and cook gently over low heat, stirring continuously, until the temperature of the custard reaches about 175°F and it is thick enough to coat the back of a spoon. Run your finger down the spoon; it should leave a clear trail. Immediately pass the sauce through a wire-mesh conical sieve into a clean bowl. Leave to cool at room temperature, stirring occasionally to stop the sauce coagulating and a skin from forming.

Cover the cold sauce with plastic wrap and refrigerate for up to 48 hours. Just before serving, add the snipped mint and a few drops of green mint syrup.

Caramel Sauce

Sauce caramel

This simple, delicious sauce can be served with a multitude of desserts, and can even be stirred into plain yogurt. It will keep in an airtight container in the refrigerator for several days.

Serves 6
PREPARATION TIME: 5 MINUTES
COOKING TIME: ABOUT 15 MINUTES

Ingredients:
1/2 CUP SUGAR
5 TABLESPOONS BUTTER, SOFTENED
1 VANILLA BEAN, SPLIT LENGTHWISE AND SEEDS
SCRAPED OUT WITH THE TIP OF A KNIFE
2 CUPS HEAVY CREAM

In a thick-bottomed saucepan, combine the sugar, butter, and the seeds from the vanilla bean. Set over very low heat and stir continuously with a wooden spoon until the sugar has dissolved completely. Continue to cook until the mixture turns an attractive caramel color. Immediately take the pan off the heat and stir in the cream, taking care that you are not spattered as the cold cream hits the hot caramel. Mix well and cook the sauce over medium heat for 5 minutes, stirring continuously with the wooden spoon. The sauce should be perfectly blended, pliable, and shiny. Pass it through a wire-mesh conical sieve and leave to cool at room temperature before serving.

Rum Sauce

Sauce au rhum

The perfect complement to bread pudding, Christmas plum pudding, and rum and raisin ice cream.

Serves 6
PREPARATION TIME: 5 MINUTES
COOKING TIME: ABOUT 10 MINUTES

Ingredients:
1 1/4 CUPS HEAVY CREAM
5 TABLESPOONS SUGAR
2 TEASPOONS CORNSTARCH MIXED WITH
2 TABLESPOONS MILK
1/3 CUP DARK RUM (PREFERABLY CAPTAIN MORGAN
OR NEGRITA)
2 TABLESPOONS GOLDEN RAISINS, BLANCHED,
REFRESHED, AND DRAINED

Put the cream and sugar in a small saucepan and bring to a boil over low heat. Add the cornstarch, stirring as you go, and bubble for 2 minutes, then pour in the rum. Simmer the sauce for 2 minutes longer. Stir in the raisins and serve piping hot.

Light Chocolate Sauce

Sauce au chocolat légère

This light sauce has a good bitter chocolate flavor. It is easy to prepare and is satisfyingly low in calories. Serve it in ladlefuls with profiteroles, ice creams, and pear desserts.

Serves 6
PREPARATION TIME: 10 MINUTES
COOKING TIME: ABOUT 5 MINUTES

Ingredients:
1 CUP + 2 TABLESPOONS UNSWEETENED COCOA
POWDER
3/4 CUP SUGAR
1 1/2 CUPS WATER
1 1/2 TABLESPOONS BUTTER, SOFTENED

Combine the cocoa, sugar, and water in a saucepan and whisk until well amalgamated. Bring to a boil over low heat, whisking continuously, and boil for 2 minutes. Whisk in the butter, a little at a time, and cook for another 2 minutes. Serve the sauce immediately or keep it warm in a *bain-marie* for a few minutes.

Rich Chocolate Sauce

Sauce au chocolat riche

This rich, velvety sauce is ideal spooned over vanilla or coffee ice cream or meringues filled with whipped cream. Memories of childhood...

Serves 6
PREPARATION TIME: 10 MINUTES
COOKING TIME: ABOUT 5 MINUTES

Ingredients:
7 OUNCES BEST-QUALITY BITTERSWEET CHOCOLATE
OR *COUVERTURE*, CHOPPED
2/3 CUP MILK
2 TABLESPOONS HEAVY CREAM
2 1/2 TABLESPOONS SUGAR
2 TABLESPOONS BUTTER, DICED

Put the chocolate in a bowl and gently melt it over a pan of simmering water, stirring with a wooden spoon until very smooth. Combine the milk, cream, and sugar in a saucepan, stir with a whisk, and bring to a boil. Still stirring, pour the boiling milk mixture onto the melted chocolate, then return the mixture to the pan and bubble it for a few seconds, stirring continuously. Remove from the heat and add the butter, a little at a time, whisking until the sauce is smooth and homogeneous. Pass it through a wire-mesh conical sieve and serve hot.

White Chocolate Sauce with Mint

Sauce au chocolat blanc et à la menthe

The mint adds freshness to this sauce, which is ideal for making a marriage of two chocolate sauces with a selection of all-chocolate desserts. It is also delicious served over dark chocolate ice cream with a few pistachios scattered on top.

Serves 6
PREPARATION TIME: 10 MINUTES
COOKING TIME: ABOUT 5 MINUTES

Ingredients:
8 OUNCES WHITE *COUVERTURE* OR BEST-QUALITY
WHITE CHOCOLATE, CHOPPED
1/2 CUP MILK
1 CUP HEAVY CREAM
3 TABLESPOONS FRESH MINT LEAVES
1 TEASPOON CARAWAY SEEDS

Put the white chocolate in a bowl, stand it in a *bain-marie*, and melt it gently over low heat, stirring with a wooden spoon until smooth.

In a saucepan, bring the milk and cream to a boil. As soon as it begins to bubble, toss in the mint leaves and caraway seeds, remove from the heat, and cover the pan. Leave to infuse for 10 minutes, then strain the milk mixture through a wire-mesh conical sieve onto the melted chocolate. Mix with a whisk until thoroughly amalgamated.

Transfer the chocolate sauce to a clean saucepan, set over medium heat, and bubble for a few seconds, whisking continuously. Serve the sauce hot. If you are not serving it immediately, you can keep it warm in a *bain-marie* for a few minutes.

Matching sauces with ingredients

In this section you will find sauces designed to match whichever main ingredient you already have in your pantry or refrigerator, or which takes your fancy when you do your food shopping. Now you need no longer wonder how to add interest to vegetables, pasta, fish, meat, or fruit – just consult this index; you will find the perfect partner for whatever you plan to cook.

Index

Page numbers in *italic* refer to the illustrations